The
BRIDE'S
MANIFESTO

McDougal & Associates

Servants of Christ and stewards of the mysteries of God

"On the landscape of current ministry, there are those who stand out like an ensign of our times. It must have been what Gideon or David looked like in their generations. They were sharp rocks that the ebb and tide of cultural and religious trends broke upon. Genevah is one of these. In a generic, tepid world, there is a vanguard of ministers, missionaries and misfits who are taking center stage. They will be the rudder to the ship of modern culture and spirituality.

"I recommend Genevah because I believe she is on the frontlines of this postmodern 'changing-of-the-guard' in current Christendom. Read her words with the resolve to be one of those mentioned above, a history maker, one who defines the age and is a sign of the times. People like Genevah must resist the temptation to conform, because they are the mile markers for us all to keep in sight as we are climbing the Mountain. Lead the charge, Genevah, and many will follow!"

Chad Taylor
Founder of Consuming Fire Ministries
Author of *Why Revival Still Tarries*

"After being in ministry for many years and having written numerous endorsements for audio recordings, it is an honor to give this endorsement for *The Bride's Manifesto*.

"As a pastor, I've met hundreds of people, but when the Lord sent Sister Genevah into our ministry, we both knew our meeting was ordained of God. I feel this is only the beginning of many great writings from this woman of God. I encourage you to glean the knowledge of warfare, understanding what this book provides, and allow the Holy Spirit to help you achieve greater victories in your walk with God."

Ricky C. Perkins
Sr. Pastor, Deliverance Center of Georgia
Host of "In His Time" TV Program
Author and publisher of 200+ Christian songs
Dove Award Finalist for "Song Of The Year"
and "Album Of The Year" 2000

"Genevah is living proof of prophetic fulfillment that everyday men and women living in the conflicts of reality can become powerbrokers of Heaven. God has used an earthen vessel to reveal that His faithfulness, His love and His promises are indeed *'yea and amen.'* Genevah will take you from the everyday struggles of life and death, pain and suffering, to joy and blessing in the Kingdom of God for those who remain faithful.

"I recommend that you read this book with an open heart. It is a deep well of refreshing revelation from someone whose walk has traversed the muddy reality of the trenches, to peer from beneath the veil of the Bride to see her King. It is time for *The Bride's Manifesto* to be revealed."

Eddie T. Rogers
Revival In Power Ministries
Author of *The Power of Impartation* and
Supernatural: Living Under an Open Heaven
∽

"Over the past several years since I first met Genevah on our ministry network, my life has been thoroughly blessed and enriched by the experiences and revelations that she has shared with us on the deeper truths of the Spirit of God. I truly respect and appreciate the call and anointing of God that she walks in and the maturity that has been demonstrated in and through her life.

"I highly recommend Genevah and her inspiring book, because I believe that she has been raised up by the Lord to be on the cutting edge of what He desires to do on the earth during this great transition that is now taking place throughout the global Body of Christ. Within the pages of this book, you will come to a new and fresh understanding of the Bride of Christ and what her mandate is for the endtimes. Those who are hungry and thirsty for God, desiring a more intimate relationship with Him, have much to gain from the writings within these pages."

L.D. Oxford
Missionary Evangelist/Teacher
Founder and Overseer,
Joshua Apostolic Prophetic Network and E-list

Manifesto: "a public declaration of intentions, opinions, objectives, or motives, as one issued by a government, sovereign, or organization"

(www.dictionary.com)

The
BRIDE'S
MANIFESTO

Accepting Our Marching Orders

by
Genevah

Unless otherwise noted, all Scripture quotations are from the Authorized King James Version of the Bible. Portions marked "TLB" are from *The Living Bible* paraphrased by Kenneth Taylor, copyright © 1971 by Tyndale House Publishers, Inc., Wheaton, Illinois. References marked "NKJ" are from *The New King James Version of the Bible*, copyright © 1979, 1980, 1982, by Thomas Nelson, Inc., Nashville, Tennessee. References marked "NLT" are from *The New Living Translation of the Bible*, copyright © 1996 by Tyndale House Publishers, Inc., Wheaton, Illinois.

Original cover graphic by Christy Teresa Moss,
windwalker1@vodamail.co.za

Cover design by Sherie Campbell
sonandshield@comcast.net

Published by:

McDougal & Associates
www.thepublishedword.com

McDougal & Associates is dedicated to the spreading of the Gospel of Jesus Christ to as many people as possible in the shortest time possible.

ISBN 13: 978-1-934769-14-0
ISBN 10: 1-934769-14-2

Printed in the United States of America
For Worldwide Distribution

Acknowledgments

I want to express my heartfelt gratitude and appreciation to my family and friends who've loved me unconditionally and have been so instrumental in my life's journey. I'm sure they must have questioned my sanity at times. Also, God has sent many anointed pastors, teachers, evangelists, prophets and apostles to help illuminate my pathway, as I've searched for my purpose in life.

Within the pages of this book, I have acknowledged several saints, some well-known and others unknown to the public. These people have been key players in my journey, as I approached strategic crossroads. It is not my intent to lift any of them up for their accomplishments, only to express gratitude for their obedience to our Lord and Master in operating within the parameters of their calling. Therefore, I have purposely chosen *not* to mention specific names in this portion of the book.

There's a biblical warning concerning false teachers that we must all heed: *"...their mouth speaketh great swelling words, having men's persons in admiration because of advantage"* (Jude 1:16). Although I'm certainly not a Bible scholar, nor a gifted teacher, this verse makes me very keenly aware of the dangers in how we esteem people. There is room for only one King on the throne of our hearts, and it should always be Jesus Christ! There is only One who is worthy of our praise. David sang, *"I will call upon the LORD, who is worthy to be praised"* (Psalm 18:3). I agree.

Jesus said, *"And I, if I be lifted up from the earth, will draw all men unto me"* (John 12:32). Although one facet of the truth found in this verse signified what death He would die, my prayer is that Jesus, at this very moment, is drawing all men unto Himself, because we are lifting Him up in these pages. May each of us have the love and boldness to publicly acknowledge that Jesus Christ is Lord over our lives, our families, our churches, our communities and our countries. Indeed, He is Lord over the whole Earth!

Contents

About the Cover

"When I finally left the Chamber that day, I looked down to find that I was wearing a beautiful wedding garment, but, for some reason, I couldn't move my feet. When I lifted the garment to try to discover the reason, I saw it immediately. Underneath that beautiful garment, I was wearing heavy combat boots!" (From Chapter 5)

This is the essence of the cover. This Bride is made up of laborers and warriors; however it's the Lord's battle. And gifts are being released to His Bride, as she prepares the way for the return of her Bridegroom.

FOREWORD BY
DR. WINSTON MOSS

There are many prolific authors in the world today, some of them churning out great volumes to the complete satisfaction of their readership. There are not nearly as many, though, laboring as underground rivers, in almost total obscurity, never merely for the satisfaction of their readers. Theirs is the strong labor of love, born out of the painful isolation of their own personal life experiences. Their walk with Christ has afforded them great insight into the things that assail the lives of mankind. Theirs is a unique spiritual sightedness of prophetic vision, a deep and accurate spiritual focus and a total commitment to the Word and the ways of God.

Genevah is one of these special gifts to the Body of Christ. She moves in a high level of insight and revelation, she writes only what she lives, and she speaks only with the authority of a sent one. Her life itself is an open book. Although she possesses a beautiful and wise mind, the mind of Christ remains her source of wisdom and knowledge. *"From a wise mind comes careful and persuasive speech"* (Proverbs 16:23, TLB). Every one of her many achievements has become the incense she willingly burns to the glorifying of her God and heavenly Father.

Within the pages of *The Bride's Manifesto* you will find answers to the perplexing questions concerning Christ and His beautiful Bride. It is my personal desire to see Genevah produce a great number of books that will teach us how to live to the fullest extent of God's will for us all. Well done, good and faithful servant. Enter into your destiny!

Dr. Winston Moss,
Resurrection Life Ministries
Port Elizabeth, Republic of South Africa

INTRODUCTION

Much is being said these days about this season of the Bride and the Bridegroom. It is my earnest prayer that you will find encouragement, enlightenment and enjoyment within the pages of this book. In it I have shared some of my most intimate experiences in my walk with the Lord, not for the sake of boasting or of airing any dirty laundry, but simply to show how God uses ordinary people to demonstrate His extraordinary love. Hopefully, what I've shared will challenge you to desire a personal encounter with Christ. Should you disagree with any of the contents of this book, that's your prerogative. However, I still love being "wowed" by my awesome God, and I hope you will enjoy it too.

A dream I had in the early 1970s, in which I was suddenly awakened while reading my own obituary, caused such an impact on my life that I began a quest for God and the truth about Heaven and Hell. On February 4, 1983, I found the Truth and asked Jesus Christ to come into my life and be the Lord of it. From that moment on, my life has never been the same.

"A gift is as a precious stone in the eyes of him that hath it: whithersoever it turneth, it prospereth" (Proverbs 17:8). This verse became my daily prayer for God to supernaturally prosper my gift of salvation. It was and still is *"as a precious stone"* to me, and I desire for the testimony of my life to be my gift to Him.

Through the veil, I can see His face in the distance. My heart pants passionately for Him, and I long for the day when that veil is lifted and I gaze into His face. As I reflect on the memories of my walk down the aisle of destiny, nostalgia floods my soul, and I'm reminded of those who've gone on before and those who will come after me. The prayer of my heart is for them *all* to be present on that great day.

There's room in my Father's house for more. Will you join us center stage as we corporately position ourselves for the finale of the greatest story ever told?

Jesus said, *"I am the way"* (John 14:6). All of Heaven awaits this spectacular event in honor of the King of Glory. We're the Father's gift to His beloved Son! This, then, is *The Bride's Manifesto*.

His Handmaiden,
Genevah

P.S. Some might ask what I know of brides or weddings. I married the night after my graduation from high school and had four sons. (My first son, David, died when he was just sixteen days old.) That marriage ultimately failed because neither of us knew Christ. I married again later in life, and we were very much in love. After many years and many struggles, however, that marriage failed too, this time because I *had* come to know Christ, and my husband was not happy about that fact. Now Jesus is my husband, and every day I reach for a closer walk with Him.

CHAPTER 1

THE MISSION

*If ye be reproached for the name of Christ, happy are ye;
for the spirit of glory and of God resteth upon you: on their
part he is evil spoken of, but on your part he is glorified.*

1 Peter 4:14

"Hey! We heard you're praying for people. Can you pray
for me?"

Oh, Jesus, was it *really* happening, those things we had
prayed so earnestly for, that people would come running to us
because of sensing Your glory?

In Awe!

Joanie Erickson and I sat in awe, as a young man poured out his heart to John Crowder, telling him of the surgery he just had on his shoulder and the second surgery he was facing. He told John that his father was a pastor but that he himself had been away from God. As John took the young man's hand and began praying for him, Joanie and I laid hands on him and also prayed.

After prayer, John told the young man that Jesus had healed his arm, and there would be no need for the second surgery. The young man began moving that arm wildly—affirming the fact that the Lord had indeed touched him.

He then asked John if he would "save" his friend, who had been wanting to get saved for a long time. As the other young man bowed his head and prayed for Jesus to come into his heart and save him, Joanie and I began praising the Lord for what He was doing in that place.

Hard to Believe

It was still hard to believe what was happening. I had been talking to John about the supernatural healings and other miracles that Eddie Rogers (of Revival in Power) was experiencing at a food bank in Bremen, Georgia, when the young man had approached us and literally broken into our conversation with his request for prayer. John told us about others who had come up to him before these two young men, asking for prayer for salvation, healing and wanting deliverance from homosexuality.

The interesting thing is that we were not sitting in a church building, nor were we having a church service. We were actually sitting in a *hookah* bar in Stockton, California, owned by Muslims. Such bars have become enticing gathering places for teens and college-age kids, a place where they can "hang out" with friends and smoke flavored tobacco through water pipes. (Parents, make sure that flavored tobacco is the only thing your kids are smoking!)

A fairly large group of us were there, split up into small groups, talking with the young people. We had left The Father's House after an intense encounter with the Glorious One during more than three hours of intense prophetic praise and worship. The prophetic words released there through Chad Taylor (of Consuming Fire Ministries) and John Crowder (of Sons of Thunder) over cities and countries that spanned the globe helped raise the spiritual climate to such a degree that many of us felt there had to be a release, or we would explode, and our encounter at the *hookah* bar was the result.

This is where, I believe, many Christians are missing the mark. When we ascend into the heavenly realm of the Lord's glory, what we receive is not for us to take home and bask in. Instead, we need to take it to the streets. This is the anointing Peter was walking in that caused lives to be changed as he simply passed people in the street. When we are changed from glory to glory, we can then become catalysts of change for others, through the Spirit of God's glory that rests upon us!

SEEKING RADICAL CHANGE

If you want to see radical changes in your own life, find what many of us have come to call a "provoker prophet" and get connected to him or her. I watched Chad Taylor provoke the youth worship team at The Father's House on Sunday night, not really understanding what he was doing and yet intrigued by it. Just when they all thought the powerful service was over, Chad grabbed a water drum and began provoking them into a higher realm of praise and worship. Although some people had begun leaving, others stopped to behold this wonder.

Spontaneous prayer and worship began breaking out in pockets all over the church. "Sonshine" Matheney took a picture of the worship team with her digital camera, and it revealed a huge lion's head with fire blazing from it that almost covered Chad. Breakthroughs were sensed simultaneously by the members of the worship team. Although they walked away from the experience exhausted, several of them with blisters on their fingers and hands from the intensity and duration of their playing, they knew that something wonderful had happened in the spirit realm over Stockton that night!

Later, after returning to Georgia, I received an e-mail from Chad. He said the local news media had somehow heard about the prophetic words that were being released and wanted to send a camera crew to The Father's House for an interview.

Shortly before going to California, John had visited the United Kingdom. He decided to take a small group out onto the streets. Rather than preach, they would just worship and get into the glory and then see what the Holy Spirit would do through them. Within a few minutes, people started coming up to them, wanting to get saved and wanting what they had. When they were specifically asked, then they told the seekers about Jesus. In less than two hours, thirty people had been saved, without any of the team having preached a word. They simply cast the net where the Holy Spirit led them, and the "little fishes (as John described them) just jumped in!"

CREATIVE MIRACLES

It's very exciting to hear about the creative miracles that

are happening in diverse gatherings where the Glorious One is appearing. John told of someone in one of his recent services who was able to see through a glass eye. Eddie and several others at his food bank gatherings recently witnessed a lady's "shorter" leg grow to the same length as her other leg. It has to be God when every person who's prayed for in a food bank gets healed!

After watching Chad Taylor provoke the youth group into a powerful breakthrough, my prayer is that this book will provoke a group of remnant warriors to get out of their comfort zones and determine to become "water walkers!" Unless you are willing to take risks that no one else is willing to take, you will be a drifter all your life in your little-bitty boat of fear.

A POWERFUL VISION

There's no way I can ever go back to church as usual after what I experienced in California. Hearing John Crowder share his wife Lily's powerful vision that God gave her for the West side of Atlanta has stoked a fire that was already blazing deep within my bones. Lily saw silver bridges over three cities—Douglasville, Dallas and Carrollton. According to www.tehila.org, the biblical meaning of *silver* is: "Understanding; knowledge; purity; cleanliness; redemption; words of God; promises of God; cleansed and ready for use; very precious to God." The biblical meaning of *bridge* is: "communication and union; connection between God and man; an ascension; the end of one cycle and the beginning of another. In many cultures it is the link between what can be perceived and what is beyond perception; a change or desire for change."

If you happen to live in one of those three cities, and that doesn't do something to your spirit, you may need to check to see if you're even saved. The glory of God is already here. Just pray for the Holy Spirit to open your eyes to it. Maybe the god of this world has blinded your eyes and made you believe the lie that we're just waiting on God to pour out His glory. No! He's waiting on us!

Personally, I want to be one of those bridges. I also want to be a burning bush. How about you? And if you live somewhere else, this is for you too. This next great move of God is for the corporate Body, not just for one man or one ministry. Get on board the Holy Ghost Express and enjoy the ride of a lifetime! *"And one cried unto another, and said, Holy, holy, holy, is the Lord of hosts: the whole earth IS full of his glory"* (Isaiah 6:3, Emphasis Mine).

JESUS IS LORD OVER ...

One day this spring, I needed to drive into Carrollton for a personal matter, and I was led to take a different route than usual. As I was approaching the city, I couldn't believe my eyes. There was a huge billboard that read, "JESUS is LORD Over Carrollton." That made such an impact on me that I nearly slammed on my brakes. Immediately I cried out, "Jesus, when this book comes out, I want a billboard ministry."

Later that week, I told my friend Winston Moss about seeing the billboard and about asking Jesus for a billboard ministry. He told me about a man in Houston, Texas, who also had a billboard ministry several years ago. No one could figure out how he was able to finance billboards all over the Houston area declaring that Jesus was Lord over that great city.

Although I realize that John Osteen's life and ministry had a major impact on his son Joel, this made me wonder if those billboards might have been another key to the location of Joel's ministry, one that is currently impacting lives globally.

For my part, I'm longing to see signs all around the perimeter in our city declaring, "JESUS is LORD Over Atlanta," not to mention all the smaller cities on the outskirts! You can believe for the same thing to happen in your city.

CREATED FOR WORSHIP

God created us for His pleasure but also to worship Him. The more you worship, the closer you get to God, and the closer you get to God, the more you want to worship Him. I love what John Bevere, in a sermon at Trinity Chapel Church of God, said the Lord told him: "Worship is not a slow song." He also made this statement in his book, *Drawing Near: A Life of Intimacy with God* (Nashville, Thomas Nelson Publishers: 2004). According to *Webster's Dictionary*, *worship* simply means "to show extravagant respect or admiration to an object of esteem." Just adore *Him* and declare who *He* is!

I also heard a *rhema* word from Robin Bolin that I've never forgotten. She said that when Satan made the three attempts to get Jesus to bow down to him, it was worship that made him leave Jesus for a season. If you want to send the rascal running, just start worshiping the Lord. You don't need a CD or a worship team from church to set the atmosphere for your worship. You can do it by the attitude of your heart. And you can do it anywhere, even sitting at your desk at work! Learn the names/natures of Jehovah, so that you can declare who He is in your life!

ANOTHER CHAPTER

While I was in California, I discussed this book with Chad, thinking that I'd almost completed the final chapter, which I called "The Mandate." Chad told me I needed to write one more chapter, "The Mission." I was puzzled by that because I thought that *mission* would be redundant with *mandate*. After looking up both words in *Webster's Collegiate Dictionary*, I better understood his reasoning:

- *Mandate*: "An authoritative command"
- *Mission*: "A definite military, naval or aerospace task, a flight operation of an aircraft or space craft in the performance of a mission, calling"

When I read that, instantly I reflected back on the plea that had gone forth from my lips in the year 2000. I had asked the Lord to please put me in boot camp and train me in all branches of His special forces. I was willing to start out as a foot soldier, but eventually I wanted assignments in His air force, with authority over the principalities and rulers that were reigning over my city and holding the people in captivity.

Such assignments must be accomplished on a corporate level in Atlanta, and it will only be achieved through unity in diversity, because we are contending for the now huge Metro Atlanta area, not just for the City of Atlanta itself! And you must hear God's call for your city as well. I'm convinced that *"the latter rain"* of which the Bible speaks is about revival for the entire Body of Christ, so get ready for it.

WHAT GOD IS SAYING

Recently, we were in the heat of revival at Deliverance Center of Georgia with pastors Eddie Mereliz and Ricky Perkins and their families. I spent most of one day fasting and praying because I wanted to hear what the Holy Spirit was saying for our city. He told me that during the first six months of the year we would *morph* (transform). This, He told me, was necessary for preparation. Then, He said, the final six months of the year we would *mobilize* (assemble and make ready for war). This was necessary for purpose. "You are sensing the heat of revival," He said, "but you must contend for it!"

I looked up a few of these words;

- *Heat,* I found, has more than one meaning. Beyond mere temperature, it means: "A single continuous effort; one of several preliminary contests held to eliminate less competent contenders." This is a spiritual competition, and we're contending for territories.
- *Contend*: "Maintain, assert."
- *Maintain*: "To sustain against opposition; uphold or defend; to persevere."
- *Assert*: "To declare forcefully or aggressively; to compel recognition of one's rights."
- *Compel*: "To drive forcefully by overcoming pressure."

I'm reminded of the words of Jesus: *"And from the days of John the Baptist until now the kingdom of heaven suffereth violence, and the violent take it by force"* (Matthew 11:12).

OUR MOABs

Recently I've been hearing in the Spirit phrases like "the 4th of July," "Independence," "Peachtree Road Race," "pivotal" (meaning "vitally important, crucial") and "point" (a verb, meaning "to give added force; separate; direct someone's attention to; to train for a particular contest.") The apostle Paul wrote: *"I press toward the mark for the prize of the high calling of God in Christ Jesus"* (Philippians 3:14). I don't believe it's mere coincidence that the annual Peachtree Road Race here in Atlanta is attracting runners from many nations. Nor do I believe it was mere coincidence that Atlanta was chosen for the Summer Olympics in 1996. God is up to something in our city concerning the nations, and this is now the twelfth year (apostolic fullness) since those historic games were held.

A New Level of Warfare

The level of warfare I've experienced, from the moment I sat down to begin writing this book, has been extraordinary. I've had to force my way through enemy territory. My friend Winston Moss is also writing a book, one that is almost a parallel to this, but his is on a much deeper level and in greater detail. He said the Lord told him that our books would be two of many that would be weapons of mass destruction in these end times. We're praying, in agreement, that these are "spiritual MOABs" given by the Holy Spirit from the Lord's arsenal. (For those who don't know, MOAB is an acronym for the most powerful weapon in the United States' arsenal, in the words of Saddam Hussein, "the Mother of All Bombs!")

Have you been experiencing a lot of "flack" recently for your love for Christ? Do you wonder why people are starting to treat you as if you had a communicable disease? Have you been crying out to the Lord, asking Him what's wrong with you? My friend, it's not what's *wrong,* but what's *right* with you.

Look for Him in Everything

Another word the Lord recently gave me has made a major impact on the way I now see things. He said, "Look for Me in everything; quit looking for the enemy behind anything." Immediately I saw the words "lesson or blessing." A friend told me I would probably find a lesson and a blessing when I started responding to everything in the way the Lord said. It's been a real challenge, but I'm trying very hard to look for God in anything that I would ordinarily have considered to be an enemy attack.

Something He revealed to me more than twenty years ago is nearly a parallel to this. He said, "Soul reacts, but spirit responds." And another great truth: "You will find whatever or whomever you're seeking or looking for!" This is a challenge for all of us.

WHAT SHOULD YOU DO?

So what should you do? Talk about your salvation experience as often as you get an opportunity. It's your testimony of God's amazing love and grace. It's something I even encouraged the homeless people in Woodruff Park to do—to tell everyone who sat down beside them that Jesus Christ had saved them. I gave them Bible tracts that had been prayed over and asked them to share the Gospel with everyone who would listen. Whether or not they could read themselves seemed unimportant. I knew there was power in the Gospel they would carry!

It was amazing how the Lord blessed our ministry in that park. We even had a police officer who watched over us. A nearby café owner asked that officer to let us know we were welcomed in her place of business to witness to people. This same officer told us to let the ones who wanted to attend services at our rescue mission know that he would pay for them to ride the MARTA bus there if they came back on Sunday. How wonderful!

IT'S TIME TO GET HAPPY

The most important thing to do right now is just be happy

in the joy of the Lord. According to Jesus, your joy should be based on one thing only—that your name is written in the Lamb's Book of Life—your salvation, not your circumstances. *His* joy is *your* strength! Why not ask Him for a whole carafe, not just a sip, of His new wine and get "smashed out of your mind" and right into His mind.

Some of the happiest people in the world are drunkards. They love everybody, and they'll talk to anyone. They'll give you the clothes off their back. They don't care who is looking at them; they want to sing and dance (if they can stand up), and they don't know when to stop drinking. They just want to party all the time—especially at night, when it's the darkest outside!

An alcoholic doesn't want to get sobered up. He or she will get up in the morning and immediately start looking for another drink. Amazingly, it's these drunkards around whom everyone seems to gather in bars. People are drawn to those who are happy—no matter what their condition may be. Oh, that we would discover a remnant of real Holy Ghost drunkards, people who never want to sober up. They'll just want to have a Holy Ghost party 24/7.

Joel's Bar is a franchise that you don't need money to invest in, nor do you have to worry about code violations. All you have to do is get to know the Word that became flesh, so you'll know the authority He has given you to command your own internal water pots to fill up.

As you continue walking with this wonderful Lord by faith, your water, the water of life, will turn into new wine, and you will become a portable bar. People will come running to you, for, as Jesus promised, *"He that believeth on me, as the scripture hath said, out of his belly shall flow rivers of living water* (John 7:38).

You don't have to be in a church building to experience

the joy of your salvation; we are the church! And we are commanded to be filled with the Spirit at all times (see Ephesians 5:18). We are to *"be instant in season and out of season"* (2 Timothy 4:2). In other words, always be ready to give someone a reason for your joy and the hope that's in you.

GET FILLED UP

No one else can fill your water pot. You must fill it according to the Word of God:

- *"Speaking to one another in psalms and hymns and spiritual songs, singing and making melody in your heart to the Lord"* (Ephesians 5:19, NKJ).
- *"Giving thanks always for all things to God the Father in the name of our Lord Jesus Christ"* (Ephesians 5:20, NKJ).
- *"Submitting to one another in the fear [respect or reverence] of God"* (Ephesians 5:21, NKJ).

Your extreme joy will cause a shout from your spout that will send the enemy running in fear. He knows that your shout is a clarion call to the heavenly hosts that are coming to give him a major migraine!

This is the key to releasing corporate MOAB's. As we unite with our Jericho shouts, we become a corporate roar that will shout down any wall of adversity or division and will send the enemy running every time! Why? Because our roar is resounding between Heaven and Earth in harmony with the roar of the Lion of the tribe of Judah (like surround sound), and it has become a terrorizing alarm to the kingdom of darkness operating in the second heaven!

THE BRIDE'S MANIFESTO

Now, it's time to gain further momentum! We're now in the fourth quarter, and it's time to RRROOOAAARRR! It's time to accept *The Bride's Manifesto.*

CHAPTER 2

WHO IS THE BRIDE?

And there came unto me one of the seven angels which had the seven vials full of the seven last plagues, and talked with me, saying, Come hither, I will shew thee the bride, the Lamb's wife.   Revelation 21:9

As a child, I believe, every little girl dreams of her big day, that day when she will walk down the aisle in her beautiful, white wedding gown toward her soulmate, who awaits her at the altar. I'm sure every young woman feels that this is *the* most important event in her life. As the Body of Christ, our most important event in life is salvation, but as the Bride of

Christ, it's our upcoming wedding. Nothing could be more exciting!

THE ANALOGY OF THE WEDDING

Jesus often taught in parables, and God has given us natural analogies that can reveal spiritual principles and truths. In the wedding, we find many such analogies. For instance, you don't become a bride on the first date. Ideally, that decision is made after a healthy friendship and relationship have developed and matured. So we have a lot of maturing to do.

God's plan for the institution of marriage is covenant, to be broken only by death. Sadly, far too many people still look upon marriage as a contract, not a covenant, and because of this, that white wedding gown has lost its symbolic representation of purity. It has become little more than a fashion statement.

Let us look at some of the other parallels between the natural and spiritual in regard to the wedding, and, as we do, please take time to pause and ponder. I do that quite often, and it's amazing how the Holy Spirit will bring clarity to a principle or truth that I might be struggling with.

WHAT IS YOUR RELATIONSHIP?

What is your relationship with the Bridegroom? Are you His intimate Bride whom He cherishes? Perhaps you're the fiancé who loves Him and wants to flaunt her gifts from Him, but doesn't have the self-discipline necessary to become His Bride. Maybe you're the girlfriend who wants to tell others how super He is but doesn't want to make a personal commitment to turn loose of other lovers.

Or might you be considered the harlot, who only wants

what He can do for you? Is He just a utility switch you turn on when you need something for your pleasure? Is the Bridegroom a mere casual acquaintance, a good old boy who might be an interesting topic of conversation when you're around someone you want to impress?

Last, but certainly not least, is the One who's been waiting anxiously for you at the altar someone you've just heard other people talk about, but don't really know? With many, this is surely the case.

If the last question applies to you, please see the end of this book for your personal invitation from the Bridegroom Himself. However, if you've already accepted Jesus Christ as your personal Savior, then He desires to have an even more personal relationship with you. His desire is that you become part of His corporate Bride, as well as His corporate Body, and that takes dedication and preparation.

Revelation 21:9, our theme verse for this chapter, is the only reference in the Bible to the Bride being *"the Lamb's wife,"* and what is being described there takes place in Heaven. That tells us something. Ultimate union with God will occur only in eternity, but down here He offers us the growing intimacy of getting to know our beloved Bridegroom.

MOVING FROM FIANCÉ TO BRIDE

When does a woman move from the role of fiancé to the role of bride? The moment she accepts an engagement ring and/or makes a public announcement that she is planning to become the wife of her future mate, she is then considered to be his fiancé or bride-to-be. And personally, I believe that's where we all start, when we've accepted Jesus as our Savior. We instantly become part of His Body, but that's not to say that we're yet aware of our completeness or fullness in Him.

That can only happen after an intimate relationship has developed and matured.

Just the opposite happens in the natural realm. True intimacy in marriage is ideally reserved for the honeymoon, after the wedding, and it's at this point that our physical bodies are united together, and we become one. During the to-be season, there is usually a flurry of activities—showers, shopping, wedding and honeymoon planning, housing considerations, schedules to be arranged, budgets to be made, dieting, etc. Fortunately, most couples have family and friends to help with these arrangements and the finances they involve. However, stress frequently creeps into the relationship at this point—due to the extreme busyness—and tempers tend to erupt.

These are perilous times in any relationship because it's so easy for doubt to come marching through the front door, and when it does, joy flees out the back. If that happens, it becomes a volatile situation. There might even be a former flame who tries to step back into your life as a comforter, or even a new acquaintance. Be careful!

This same scenario often unfolds in the life of baby Christians who are endeavoring to develop an intimate relationship with the Lord Jesus. Don't ever think that the enemy is happy about your decision to follow the Lord. On the other hand, don't ever think that you're alone. You'd be surprised at the number of comrades in your company.

Watch out for those former flames who comforted you in the past. Perhaps you had to use alcohol or drugs to relieve stress, or you used sex as a tension tamer. In some cases, it may suddenly appear that a new door is opening for you to transfer on your job and, as always, you think the grass might be greener on the other side of the fence. At this point, carefully consider any major decision, such as relocation, and seek spiritual counseling before making any such move. Oftentimes the enemy will use money as a lure to take you out of a place of spiritual growth intended to prosper your soul.

SHOWERS OF BLESSINGS NEGLECTED

Showers of blessings are given to everyone who accepts Jesus as their Savior, but for one reason or another, it often takes us a while before we recognize or open all our gifts. Sadly, some of them are actually abandoned as unappreciated. It's terribly heartbreaking to see people walking away from the most precious gift of all—salvation—when we know that the Holy Spirit is moving in their hearts. If they would just sit down and consider how very long eternity is, surely they would not cast aside such a great and precious gift.

They might never again have such an opportunity before the death angel comes to visit. If you're unprepared to face the Judgment Seat of Christ immediately after your appointed time with death, please see the end of this book, so that you can settle all uncertainty and doubt before it's too late. If you have a family member or friend who's lost, there is also a powerful prayer to be found there, which you can pray for their salvation.

A SMALL WINDOW OF OPPORTUNITY

In all actuality, there's only a small window of opportunity in which a woman can be considered a bride. Even at my wedding rehearsal, I still felt like a bride-to-be because I wasn't yet arrayed in my wedding garments. It wasn't until I had stepped into that beautiful white gown that I finally felt the role. That one step caused a great change in the way I felt about myself.

I suddenly knew it was my day, the one I had waited for so long. It had finally arrived!

My gown was very simple in design, but it was so very elegant to me—twenty-five yards of white satin, hand-tailored by a very dear friend of my daddy.

When your relationship with Jesus has become so intimate that you know beyond a shadow of a doubt that you're the Bride He's coming for, it will change your life forever! The boldness you begin to walk in at that moment will empower you to be an overcomer to the very end.

From that day forward, no matter what weapon the enemy tries to form against you, it will not prosper. Your union with your heavenly Bridegroom has been arranged and ordained by your heavenly Father, and no one can change that fact!

THE FOCUS IS ON THE BRIDE

Ninety-nine percent of the focus at a wedding is always on the bride. Why is that? It's because it's her day. The most poignant moment of my own wedding came during the walk down the aisle. I had a very large hoop under my gown, and a couple of times I stumbled because the weight of the material made it cumbersome for me to walk. Without speaking a word, Daddy tightened his grip on my arm the moment he noticed my struggle. His smile let me know not to worry; he wasn't about to let me fall.

In our daily struggles, it's so comforting to know that we're being held securely by our heavenly Father. We're on a journey to the altar, where the Bridegroom is patiently awaiting His Bride. I sincerely believe that aisle represents the highway of life, where the fullness of our destiny is being walked out even now.

THE RING-BEARER

The ring-bearer in a wedding goes before the bride, with the symbol of covenant carried on a small white pillow—a picture of purity and holiness. This sacred symbol of covenant was purchased by the Bridegroom for the one who has chosen to become one with Him.

The rose petals strewn by another small child release the fragrance of the roses that had to be bruised and stripped of their beauty in order to produce their ultimate purpose. Humility is the fragrance of Christ, and I believe this analogy represents our crucified life, walked out in the faith steps of a small child. It has produced such an aroma that it has gone before us and entered into His nostrils as a delight for Him to savor.

THE WITNESSES

The witnesses on both sides in a wedding watch in awe as the bride begins her walk to the altar, still veiled. Everyone focuses on the brilliance of her magnificent wedding garments and her own beauty. Each step that is taken in perfect harmony with the rising crescendo of the Wedding March, being played by skilled musicians, adds to the excitement of her approach.

At the end of the aisle, there is usually a gap near the altar. When she comes to this, it is the most frightening time for the bride. Everything and everyone is now behind her—family, friends, former lovers, the former life of freedom without commitment. She is now facing her future and the one who holds her future, and there's no turning back!

The emotional roller coaster of life reveals her final threshing floor, where the wheat is separated from the chaff. As both are thrust into the air, winds toss them furiously during the winnowing process, before they fall to the ground, the good separated from the bad. This is *"the valley of the shadow of death"* for her, the stripping process of everything and everyone who has been part of who she was. She will now be tenderly and lovingly wrapped by the very one with whom she will become complete. Her beautiful wedding gown has become swaddling clothes, for death is part of the process of life!

A Better Understanding

I trust that, with these insights, you're able to gain a better understanding of the importance of the preparation necessary to become the Bride of Christ. He's not looking for a harlot or a girlfriend who's still having affairs with the world. His pure Bride must be willing to forsake all others for Him.

Even though the marriage of the Lamb takes place in Heaven, please don't be so foolish as to think you can prepare once you get there. By then, it will be too late! You won't be able to rush down the aisle at the midnight hour, for He will no longer be waiting for you at the altar.

If you haven't already discerned just what happens at the altar, think about the moment you will see Jesus face-to-face, without the veil. Yes, that will happen the day you leave this earthly body to be with your Bridegroom forever. But the journey to the altar will not be the end of your life; that will be just the beginning!

(One of the most tragic realities of a wedding is that some who are invited come only as spectators. They have no desire to become a bride themselves!)

Seeing Jesus Now

Although the majority of Christians will see Jesus as I described above, many are seeing manifestations of Him on this side of eternity. I had encounters with Him in the Spirit during a season of visitations to the Chamber of the Bridegroom, and many others have had similar encounters. Jesse Duplantis described a powerful encounter he had with Jesus in Heaven, and when I heard it, it stirred a passion within me to have a similar encounter.

Pastor Benny Hinn told of an encounter two Muslim children had that captured the attention of local news media. The children were sealed alive in a tomb after their parents died because there was no one to care for them, but over the coming days a mysterious visitor came to speak with them and bring them food every day. Ten days later, their laughter caught the attention of someone walking through the cemetery, and immediately the authorities were called to come and open the tomb.

The children were then questioned about how they could remain alive and well for so long and who it was who had helped them. Their reply was, "His name was Jesus." We have a powerful promise from Him: *"He that hath my commandments, and keepeth them, he it is that loveth me: and he that loveth me shall be loved of my Father, and I will love him, and will manifest myself to him"* (John 14:21). Not only is Jesus manifesting Himself to those who love Him and are keeping His commandments, but He's going the extra mile in manifesting Himself, even to the heathen.

How much more, then , should we expect to see Him! Think about it. If Jesus visited His disciples during the fifty days between the resurrection and His ascension into Heaven, to encourage them and give them specific instructions concerning their destinies, don't you think it's possible that He's been doing it for each generation of disciples since then? I certainly do. And furthermore, I believe there will be an increase of such visitations the closer we get to His return.

THE HONEYMOON

Another powerful analogy in the life of the Bride who is passionate about his/her destiny is the honeymoon. Could it be possible the threshing floor that I described in a previous paragraph is actually the doorway to the threshold the Bridegroom desires to carry His Bride over on their wedding night? Once again, I searched *Webster's Dictionary* for more clues to this spiritual picture. Consider these meanings:

- *Thresh:* "separate seed from a harvested plant"
- *Threshing machine:* "separates grain crops into grain or seeds and straw"
- *Threshold:* "gate; door; end; boundary. Place or point of entering or beginning [outset] of a new age. Point at which a physiological or psychological effect begins to be produced. A level, point or value above which something is true or will take place, and below which it is not or will not."

In the natural, intimacy results in two people becoming one flesh in the eyes of God. However, in the Spirit realm, true intimacy between the Bride and Bridegroom can only occur when there's been a separation unto Him. He is the seed of life within us. It's like *His* seed becoming one with *our* seed to produce *the* seed! As this is achieved in every end-time disciple, we become the corporate end-time harvest of wheat that will choke out the tares. We are living in a new age, with new beginnings, because God is doing a new thing!

A PURPOSE

I believe there's a purpose for this higher level of intimacy between the Bride and Bridegroom, and it's not just for goose bumps or our pleasure. God has many burdens and/or visions that have not yet been fulfilled, and He's looking for spiritual surrogates to birth them through. Mary gave birth to the Seed. Now it's our time to replenish the Earth with the Seed (another analogy of the flesh that became the Word). God is simply looking for our submission to the Holy Spirit, in the attitude of Mary: *"And Mary said, Behold the handmaid of the Lord: be it unto me according to thy word"* (Luke 1:38).

Corporately, we are achieving this through constant renewal and binding of our minds to Christ. We already have kindred spirits because we're Kingdom kinfolks. Now we just need kindred minds. As more of the Word is engrafted into us, it becomes so much a part of us that we are changed, and others are able to see the evidence of it without us having to say a word. That sounds to me like what Peter experienced with his shadow.

Men As Part of the Bride?

The concept of men becoming the Bride may be difficult for some to identify with, but with God there is no gender. You men must have the mind of Christ in order to feel comfortable looking at yourself as a bride. We desperately need our men to find their proper place.

I have suffered through the years, not having a husband who accepted his role as spiritual leader in our home. This caused many attacks to come against me, as I took this place, standing in the gap for my family and friends. I've since been told that many Christian women suffer from fibromyalgia because they're caught up in spiritual warfare intended for their husbands, and I can believe it. I personally suffered with such horrendous pain from this disorder in 1998 that I prayed many nights for the Lord to take me home.

The Lord showed me something very interesting in 2006 about authority in the home. I saw four "P's" in the purpose of the hierarchy of authority in marriage: Provision, Protection, Presence and Peace. The husband of the home should be concerned with the first two, and the wife should focus on the last two. When the two are in perfect balance, this creates harmony in the home.

HARMONY IN THE HOME

The home is the wife's domain, and it's her responsibility to set the atmosphere and keep it "clean." When you're fervently seeking God's presence and shalom (peace) through prayer and praise and worship daily, it makes a definite difference. Such harmony can still be accomplished for a woman who is single, divorced or widowed. If she will continue focusing on the presence and peace, and lay the burden of provision and protection at the feet of Jesus, harmony will fill her home. In essence, Jesus will be a husband to her, and God will be a Father to her children. Certainly He far exceeds any expectations she could have from an earthly husband or they could have from an earthly father. I sincerely believe that God gives a special measure of grace and provision in these situations.

I realize how difficult it is for working mothers and wives today to maintain an intimate relationship with the Lord, while trying to balance all their other responsibilities. At this writing, I'm sixty-four, I've been in the public workplace now for more than forty-five years, and I've worn many different hats. But I know it can be done—if you're willing to pursue it.

When I'm at home, I love to read my Bible and pray, and I spend quality time with the Lord in praise, worship and prayer during my hundred-and-twenty-mile daily commute back and forth to work. This amounts to three to four hours on the days I work. Then, many times, during my work day, I pray silently in the Holy Ghost while sitting at my desk. My co-workers laugh, but whenever we have a serious problem that we need an immediate answer to, I head for the ladies' restroom and make it my private prayer closet. They always know that when I return I'll be bringing a solution with me.

I'm actually semiretired, but I still do contract work several days a week. As this book goes to its final edit, I've been forced again into a position of single parent raising two adopted daughters. I'm moving somewhat slower than I used to, but I don't recall ever seeing a bride run down the aisle to the altar. God wants to walk with us daily, just as He did with Adam and Eve. His gift to us is His precious Son, and we are His gift to His precious Son!

WHAT ABOUT YOU?

What about you? Are you caught up in such a flurry of busyness that you've failed to understand Who is waiting for you at the altar and why He's there? Don't miss the wedding, nor disregard the importance of His personal invitation to you. *"Now is the day of salvation"* (2 Corinthians 6:2). You're standing on the edge of eternity, the most dangerous position you could ever be in ... if you don't yet know Christ as your personal Savior.

What will you do with your invitation? Accept it? Or reject it? Think about it! Our God requires an R.S.V.P., and whether you realize it or not, if you fail to accept Jesus Christ as your Lord and Savior, then by default, you have rejected Him.

Don't miss the altar call, the moment when the Holy Spirit is tugging at your heart. You will face Jesus sooner or later, and you will bow down to Him and confess that He is Lord!

"Wherefore God also hath highly exalted him, and given him a name which is above every name: that at the name of Jesus every knee should bow, of things in heaven, and things in earth, and things under the earth; and that every tongue should confess that Jesus Christ is Lord, to the glory of God the Father" (Philippians 2:9-11).

Why not make the decision today to meet Him face-to-face as your Bridegroom instead of your Judge. There is no grace or mercy for procrastinators—only judgment! *"And as it is appointed unto men once to die, but after this the judgment"* (Hebrews 9:27).

It's time to accept *The Bride's Manifesto.*

CHAPTER 3

THE CHAMBER OF THE BRIDEGROOM

The heavens declare the glory of God.
Which is as a bridegroom coming out of his chamber, and
rejoiceth as a strong man to run a race.

Psalm 19:1 and 5

In 2002, after meditating over a teaching series by Pastor Benny Hinn concerning the victorious life of the believer, I was drawn to the cross once again. I was hungry for a deeper relationship with the Lord and desired a greater revelation of His death, burial and resurrection. For some reason, I felt compelled to start taking daily communion during this season.

THE BRIDE'S MANIFESTO

The Revelation of the Chamber

Early one morning, after reading my Bible and praying quietly for a few moments, I noticed a lot of sudden distractions. It seemed as if I had an invisible audience, and it made me feel very uncomfortable, almost like someone was spying on me. The harder I tried to ignore this "presence," the more irritating it became. Finally, in a sense of total frustration and defeat, I got up and started getting dressed for work.

I began seeking the Holy Spirit for answers as to what exactly had happened that morning and how to prevent it the next time. Although I didn't hear an audible answer, I felt an impression in my spirit: "worship."

The next morning I started out once again on my pursuit of the cross, but this time I was armed with a tape player, headphones and some powerful worship music. I got so lost in worship that it really didn't matter if anything else happened that morning.

And then it happened: as I was flowing with the heavenly music in the Spirit, I saw an open door and heard a summons to enter in.

Entering the Chamber

Upon entering, I sensed that I was standing in the very Chamber of the Bridegroom. At first, when I realized that it was His Chamber (and to me *chamber* meant *bedroom*), I was terrified at the thought that I had been deceived. A bedroom, after all, is a place for sexual intimacy. Fear gripped my heart, and thoughts bombarded my mind. Had I been deceived by seducing spirits that caused a door to open into some demonic area? Then, just as suddenly, I was thrust back into the natural realm.

I was so shaken by this experience that I prayed earnestly for the Holy Spirit to show me the truth. Where exactly had I been? And why? Once again, I did not receive an audible answer, but rather felt the impression: "dictionary." I looked up the word *chamber* in my *Merriam-Webster's Collegiate Dictionary* and found the following definition: "the reception room of a person of rank or authority." So that's what His Chamber was!

Although it was too late that morning to seek another visit to the Chamber, I sensed that there would be another opportunity. I basked in what I had experienced so far and spent a lot of time expressing my gratitude for the things God was allowing me to see.

MY LONG JOURNEY OUT OF BONDAGE

It had been a long journey out of religious bondage. Most of my church life had been spent in denominations tied to religious doctrines and traditions of men that did nothing but make life miserable. In fact, what they offered resembled "church death" more than "church life." Now all that was changing. The following morning I began a season of visitations to the Chamber of the Bridegroom that lasted about six weeks.

In the beginning, the visits were very similar and quiet. In fact, no words were spoken during the entire six weeks.

The chamber was hazy, yet I sensed a presence I knew was the Lord. During one visit, the haze seemed to vanish, and I opened my eyes to see Jesus standing there smiling at me. His peace began to permeate my entire being, as He gazed into my eyes with such love that I didn't want to leave. I had never felt so much love in my life.

During another visit, I suddenly found myself dancing

with Jesus. The music we danced to was beautiful, high-energy, Davidic music. Although I knew the room was filled with others, I only had eyes for Him. After a while, we began to twirl, faster and faster, until we were twirling so fast we became one, much like an entwined rope. When this happened, instantly I woke up, or came to myself, and stood up.

I was so drunk I could hardly walk. Back on earth now, I heard a small voice speaking into my spirit, saying, "David danced *before* Me, but I want to dance *with* you. Enter into My joy!"

There were other visitations during the six weeks that are discussed in later chapters. In this chapter, I would like to concentrate just on these early visits. This was my first experience with a season of visitations, and the Lord showed me that they were for a purpose—not just for my pleasure.

RECEIVING AND THEN GIVING LOVE

God is many things, but the one thing I experienced first-hand during those powerful life-changing visitations was His boundless love for me. I believe that He desires for us to freely give that type of love to others, just as He freely gives it to us. And you can't give something you haven't yet received.

There are multitudes in the Body of Christ who don't yet know how to minister unconditional love to others, and the reason is that they don't yet know how to receive God's unconditional love for themselves. It's my earnest prayer that if anyone reading this book is struggling in this particular area, you'll seek a divine encounter with the Bridegroom. Let Him pour His love into you and heal your wounds. God promises that if you seek Him, you *will* find Him!

No matter how much you read the Bible and attend church, if you're a hungry Christian, you'll not be satisfied with just the written, or *logos,* Word and someone else's revelation of Christ. There comes a time in your walk with Him when you want a personal encounter with Jesus that will change your life and do it "right now!"

God doesn't want us to wait until we get to Heaven to receive everything He has for us. He said: *"Eye hath not seen, nor ear heard, neither have entered into the heart of man, the things which God hath prepared for them that love him. But God hath revealed them unto us by his Spirit: for the Spirit searcheth all things, yea, the deep things of God"* (1 Corinthians 2:9-10).

When Jesus was asked by His disciples how they should pray, He gave them the Lord's Prayer as their model. It says, *"Thy will be done in earth, as it is in heaven"* (Matthew 6:10), and this prayer is for us today. I don't know about anyone else, but I want to receive just as much as my heavenly Father wants to give me while I'm here on this Earth.

WHY, LORD?

One of the most important life questions I had often asked God was why He had allowed so much pain in my life. At times, I was thoroughly convinced that He must have made a mistake when He created me. There were so many defects in me that no one seemed capable of loving me "as-is." Frequent rejection had served to affirm to me that this was simply my lot in life and that I was not to expect anything better to happen in the future.

Like Jesus, I felt *"despised and rejected of men; a [woman] of sorrows, and acquainted with grief"* (Isaiah 53:3). Pain seemed to be just lurking in the shadows, waiting for an appropriate opportunity to attack me, and the worst kind of pain is emotional, because it's the one that crushes your heart. At times, my wounds were so very painful that I somehow felt like my heart was on the outside of my body, fully exposed for anyone who desired to pierce it with arrows.

It was during this season of visitations that the Lord helped me to understand why so many things had happened to me: It rains *"on the just and on the unjust"* (Matthew 5:45), *"sin entered into the world, and death by sin"* (Romans 5:12), *"the sufferings of this present time are not worthy to be compared with the glory which shall be revealed in us"* (Romans 8:18), *"For many are called, but few are chosen"* (Matthew 22:14), and much more.

THE PRICE

There's a price to be paid for the anointing. It will cost us everything to release it to others, in order to accomplish the purpose for which God intended it. We must each be willing to take our own alabaster box (our heart, where our treasure is hidden) and break it open, so that the precious anointing He has placed there can flow out. It benefits no one while it's still in the box!

If we're not willing to let God enlarge our hearts through brokenness (in order to give us bigger hearts to hold more burdens), we limit what He can accomplish through us. Heartbreaking experiences make our hearts tender and compassionate toward others who are also hurting.

When we allow Jesus to pour His healing anointing (the Balm of Gilead) into our wounds, that anointing's not for us to keep, but to give to others whom He places in our paths. They will know that we've been where they now are. As the saying goes, "Hurting people hurt people," and it takes someone who's been in their shoes to identify with their pain and be able to help them. No one else can get close enough. Only those who've already been healed can help bring healing to others!

NON-HEALING WOUNDS

Scars are usually formed when an area heals, but, for a variety of reasons, there exists what is known as a non-healing wound. I have such a wound on my upper lip, caused by a briar ripping it open while I was walking through a wooded area. Occasionally that wound will break open and begin to bleed for no apparent reason. Whenever I hear of a mother who's experiencing grief because of the sudden death of a child—whether it's SIDS, an auto accident or any other unexpected form of death—the wound in my own heart begins to bleed for her.

There's a reason for that. My sixteen-day-old son died unexpectedly of congenital heart failure in my arms in 1962 while I was feeding him. His heart literally burst when a faulty heart valve clogged. No one can say they know how you feel, if they haven't lost a child unexpectedly themselves.

I'm sorry, but losing a small child is not the same as losing a parent when they're older, or a friend who has died from a lengthy illness. *Sudden* means "without warning," and when it happens, it's devastating and it makes you sensitive to the pain others experience.

My heart grieved for weeks, and still does, for the parents of those who perished in the 9/11 tragedy, the parents of soldiers who've given their lives for our country, the parents of children who are murdered, etc. I don't know what it's like to lose a spouse suddenly, but I know there are thousands who do.

But as painful as death is, it's part of the process of life. Jesus experienced death so that He could bring us the hope of eternal life through His resurrection power. He said, *"Verily, verily, I say unto you, Except a corn of wheat fall into the ground and die, it abideth alone: but if it die, it bringeth forth much fruit"*

(John 12:24). I've learned, after many years of trying to deal with my son's death, that you can always find purpose *in* your pain. I'm currently writing another book, *Love Is Death, Burial and Resurrection,* in which I share the process of my own healing from that sudden and unexpected death and how my own suffering has enabled me to help other sufferers.

THE LASTING EFFECTS OF
MY VISITS TO THE CHAMBER

Since 2002, there has come a great onslaught of physical and emotional pain in my life, but the Lord has sustained me through it all. Whenever I take the time to reflect on those sacred moments in the Chamber, where He was imparting so much love into me, I feel His presence wrapping loving arms around me once again, and I boldly proclaim: *"No weapon that is formed against [me] shall prosper"* (Isaiah 54:17).

At times, when I feel the weightiness of life, with all the responsibility I have, I just think about our dance of romance, and soon that weightiness is replaced with giddiness. The joy of the new wine gives me a spiritual strength and high that makes me feel like a female Samson.

I've spent many wonderful hours pondering over those special visitations. Although there were a few visits to other areas, there were several to the Chamber. During those visits, I know the Lord could have healed me instantly, but He chose to do it slowly. That was the greatest demonstration of His love for me. I was so important to Him that He didn't get in a hurry! From then on, if He had never done anything else for me while I was in this earthly body, I would not have complained.

It used to amaze me that, while people like Esther, Paul, Peter and John were on God's mind, I was too. I still weep at the thought of Him taking the time to design my framework and create the steps of my destiny that will take me into an eternity with Him. Although my earthly father walked out of my life when I was just a year old (because he didn't want a family), my heavenly Father has never let me out of His sight for a moment!

THOSE WHO HAVE NEVER FELT THIS LOVE

I know there are literally thousands of women who've never felt the unconditional love of a father or husband, and my heart goes out to every one of them. It's a painful and lonely life, when all you want so desperately is just to be loved. You pour so much of yourself into others, and yet loneliness seems to be your constant companion. There are no loving arms to caress you tenderly at night, just a pillow to absorb the ocean of tears that pour out of your soul. I understand.

One Sunday morning in 1983, as I looked around at all the married and divorced women who sat alone in our church service, I asked God if He would do something so miraculous in my life that it would bring hope and encouragement to other such women. I also asked Him to make my situation that He brought me out of to be similar or worse than the situations of those women He put in my path, so that they would know that nothing was impossible to those who believed in the power and promise of His Word.

Consequently, many times during the past twenty-five years, as I cried desperately, "God, what's happening? What have I done?" I've heard Him say, "I'm answering your prayers." One of the most powerful verses in the Bible helped me through those difficult times. It says, *"Many are the afflictions of the righteous: but the LORD delivereth him out of them all"* (Psalm 34:19).

THE BRIDE'S MANIFESTO

DAY BY DAY

I learned an extremely valuable truth from a former pastor's wife, a truth that has helped me more than she will ever know. She was having difficulty dealing with the things her husband said and did to her at times, so she told the Lord she was going to begin her day by forgiving him for everything that he might do or say to hurt her *that* day. The Lord honored that prayer so quickly and so powerfully that she began increasing the increments from that *day* to that *week* and then to that *month*, etc. It wasn't long before her prayer extended into eternity. She has been through some of the worst fiery furnaces of any pastor's wife I personally know of, so I know that her prayer of faith has been tested. Although I haven't seen her in several years now, I believe in my heart that she is still walking in that same unconditional love and forgiveness.

I sincerely believe that Jesus wants to visit every one of us personally, while we're still in this earthly body. He promised that if we would seek Him, we *would* find Him.

One of the most beautiful facets of the Holy Spirit is that He reveals Jesus to us. You must begin your journey with the Holy Spirit, but once you know Jesus intimately, He will then take you to your heavenly Father.

He's *"no respecter of persons"* (Acts 10:34), and so the door to the Chamber of the Bridegroom is open for everyone who will be His Bride. Will you enter in?

It's time to accept *The Bride's Manifesto.*

CHAPTER 4

THE COURTYARD

Enter into his gates with thanksgiving, and into his courts with praise: be thankful unto him, and bless his name.

Psalm 100:4

During that period of visitations to the Chamber of the Bridegroom, I had one visitation to the Courtyard. That was the only time I had a personal encounter with the Holy Spirit, and it was frightening at first. Although I knew something was happening inside me, I also appeared to be witnessing a scene outside my body that looked like something out of Star Wars. It seemed like streaks of lightning were flowing into my body, while at the same time, fireworks were bursting forth from within me.

As I meditated on that scene and prayed for revelation, the Holy Spirit revealed a description of the breaker anointing that was almost beyond my human ability to understand. Fortunately, when we can't find words to describe a supernatural experience, He gives us a natural illustration that explains it. I soon got mine.

NEARLY LOSING ELIZABETH GRACE

On February 25, 2003, during the night, I almost lost little three-and-a-half-year-old Elizabeth Grace to the worst asthma attack she'd ever experienced. She showed no response to breathing treatments. I kept her on my chest the rest of the night and wept and prayed for her, and she survived.

After leaving the pediatrician's office the following morning with five prescriptions–three of them steroids—I made a quick stop at Sam's Club for a few items. Elizabeth had to go in with me, and in spite of her raging fever and severe coughing spells, she started singing, "Jesus Loves the Little Children." She sang it so loudly that people began walking around the corner to see her.

I was so angry at Satan by the time I got to the parking lot, that I was almost yelling at him. He was not going to steal this child's lungs. She was destined to become (in words that she herself said came from Jesus) "a Holy Ghost Jesus worship leader."

Since I'd had to miss work that day, my mother offered to keep Elizabeth, so I could go to the Wednesday morning praise and worship service at church. I knew that somehow I had to find the open heaven for her that I'd been hearing so much about. (That was also the morning of the miracle I describe in Chapter 6.)

That day I began telling people that I believed if I could just get Elizabeth to church on March 3rd and get her into our pastor's arms, she would be healed. I envisioned laying her in his arms and her being healed instantly. I began declaring that the breaker anointing had gone before her and started calling it up within my spirit so that I could transfer it to her. I also prayed for it to hit our pastor's spirit on Monday night, during our regular healing service.

My spirit went through the ozone layer when I heard that Pastor Benny Hinn, who was in Atlanta that week, had called our pastor and told him that something powerful was going to happen during the service on March 3rd. I caught that prophecy and ran with it.

MY FIRST TOUCH OF THE BREAKER ANOINTING

On February 5, 2000, a powerful deposit of the breaker anointing was transferred to me by the laying on of hands (actually one finger) of Pastor Rod Parsley. He was in Atlanta for a two-day partners' meeting.

I had been listening to Tommy Tenney's tape series on seeking the presence of the Lord for several months, and I was so hungry for God's presence and glory in my life that I was now praying radical prayers concerning death to self. I wanted God more than I wanted life itself. My constant prayer was, "God, I want to be a dead woman walking for You."

When I heard about Pastor Parsley coming to Atlanta, I asked my son Ray to go to the meetings with me, and it proved to be a life-changing experience for the both of us. We went for the Friday night service and then went back again on Saturday morning. That morning we were asked to pray in the Holy Ghost before Pastor Parsley came out to lay hands on his partners and pray for them. While I was standing in line and praying, I had a strange vision:

> I was standing over a huge cliff, with nothing but darkness below me. I could hear pitiful moans coming from the darkness, but couldn't see anyone. I held my right hand out, and instantly it touched the hand of a family member. I grabbed the hand and hurled him over my head out of the pit. Each time I held my hand out, it touched someone I knew, and I was able to hurl them over my head from out of the pit of darkness. After several were rescued from the pit, Ray touched my shoulder to let me know that Pastor Parsley was waiting for us.

THRUST SOMEWHERE ELSE

My prayer before the meetings and also while I was standing in line had been this: "God, I want a touch from You. I'm not here for blessings." I was so hungry for Him; He was all I wanted!

I closed my eyes, with my spirit crying out for God, as I approached Pastor Parsley. Ray was standing behind me, and he told me later what happened.

Pastor Parsley barely touched the middle of my forehead with his finger, but to me it felt like I had been hit by a bolt of lightening. I hit the floor so hard I remembered thinking, "He's killed me." Ray said he had to jump out of the way to keep me from knocking him down, and it took four men to drag me away from Pastor Parsley's feet so that he could pray for others standing in line.

While my body was lying there on the floor, I felt like part of me had suddenly been thrust somewhere else. I saw the brightest light shining through my eyelashes that I had ever seen in my life, and yet I was too terrified of it to open my eyes. My mind was racing with the thought that it was too holy for me to be in that place. For some strange reason, I felt that if I kept my eyes closed, no one would know I was there, and I would be safe.

After what seemed like an eternity, some men came over to help me back to my seat. I felt like I had been stripped of every emotion and that my body had been wrapped with something. Numbness overtook my entire being. I still remember thinking to myself that I wished everyone, even Pastor Parsley, would be silent. I just wanted to sit and bask in the peaceful presence that had suddenly enveloped me. It was hours before I felt normal again.

A Veritable Niagara Falls

A few days later, as I was coming home from work, I saw something I had never experienced before. It was a vision in the sky. It looked like Niagara Falls coming out of Heaven on the right side of the vision. The part that poured out of Heaven was narrow at the top but got wider and looked like rushing white water, as it got closer to the end. The foamy billows of water were huge at the base of the falls. On the left side was a very rugged-looking mountain that had a very wide base but got very narrow as it approached Heaven. The mountain and river were side by side. All of this appeared for a brief moment.

When Tommy Tenney spoke the prophecy God had given him for Atlanta in 1999, he said it looked like a membrane hovering over our city that was so thin it was about to break through with God's Glory. I wondered if that vision might have been a picture of what was now happening. Were there multitudes of Godchasers who had started out climbing the rugged mountain, seeking to break through the thin membrane to release God's glory, but had gotten so weary that they had fallen by the wayside? I began praying earnestly for the strength to be part of the remnant that made it to the top, so we could break through and see God's glory released over our city.

Keys to Revival

As I've noted already, I've had a heavy burden for the city of Atlanta since 1983. As a consequence, I poured my heart and soul out to God for two years, asking Him to please help me understand revival. I read books and listened to tapes about the great revivals of the past. Eventually I laid it all aside and asked the Holy Spirit to show me a picture of revival I could understand in the Bible.

Most of all, I wanted to know my part in helping to bring revival to my family, my church, my city, my county, and ultimately to the ends of the Earth. On Mother's Day, 1985, I sincerely believe God honored that prayer when He began revealing to me keys to revival from John 11.

Life Is Suddenly Complicated

My life suddenly got a lot more complicated when I was led to adopt two grandchildren (through marriage). They were girls, Lauren (five) and Elizabeth (just nineteen months old). I had raised three boys, so this was a major challenge for me. My once empty nest was suddenly full again.

As much as I love my girls, my heart aches for grandparents who are having to raise grandchildren—for whatever reason. During a season of their lives when there should be peace and a time of relaxation, taking care of small children on a consistent daily basis can be very burdensome. The problems are compounded when one or more of the grandparents are still having to work (as I was).

In most cases, state family assistance programs help alleviate some of the financial burden of such adoptions, but that help is usually not enough. I believe the true hearts of foster parents are revealed when they reach out to orphans, out of love rather than from the hope of any personal or financial gain that might be obtained from providing a home for them.

It's a blessing that support groups are being formed in many different community sectors to assist grandparents in this difficult season of their lives. Through such group meetings, many problems are being addressed, and helpful solutions are being implemented. Gratefully, the elementary school Elizabeth attends has recently started such a support group.

Children who've been through a lot of trauma (as a result of major transitions in their lives), are easily confused about authority figures, and personally, I believe that's one of the reasons for so many behavioral problems with such children. Rules and boundaries are major building blocks of a child's security, and there are always inconsistencies with these factors between the home, the school, the daycare, the church and other family members, etc.

Many of today's children are suffering with illnesses that require medical attention. It's so sad to see the vast number of them who suffer from ADD/ADHD or other physical/emotional disorders as a result of their mothers having taken drugs and/or smoking while they were pregnant. Elizabeth, for instance, was born with chronic asthma, and was a very sick baby when she came to live with me.

There were many sleepless nights spent trying to calm her when she would be awakened by night terrors. These weren't just bad dreams; she was being terrorized in her sleep. I began anointing her little crib and praying for angels to watch over her. I also asked the Lord to please let angels manifest in her dreams so that she wouldn't be frightened while she slept. And it happened.

SEEING ANGELS

When Elizabeth began talking, she would wake up smiling and telling me about the "lellow-haired" angels (she couldn't say yellow) that she played with on the moon clouds. The night before she turned three, she was found sitting up in her bed with her eyes closed playing patty cake. The next morning she told me about playing patty cake with the angels on the moon clouds during the night!

Occasionally, Elizabeth would tell me about seeing Jesus in her dreams. She had one dream in particular (before she was healed from asthma), where Jesus came into her bedroom and laid His hand on her and healed her. When I picked her up from daycare that Friday afternoon, she wasn't feeling well. As the night progressed, she began running an extremely high fever and had a terrible cough. After giving her some medication for the fever, I told her I would call the doctor the following morning to see if I could bring her in. I thought it might be an asthma attack, and she might need antibiotics or steroids.

Early Saturday morning, while I was waiting for the doctor's office to open, she came downstairs and climbed up in my lap. She couldn't wait to tell me about Jesus healing her and to let me know that she didn't need to go to the doctor!

DREAMING DREAMS

The dreams Elizabeth began having when she was four

years old were mind-boggling. I spent several hours talking with a lady who was very anointed in dream interpretations, and she was amazed at the prophetic nature of these dreams. She gave me some very detailed interpretations of the dreams, but the reasons she gave for them having these types of dreams made me realize that life was not going to be easy for any of us in the future.

I had grown accustomed to anointing the girls at night and asking the Holy Spirit to visit them in their dream realm. Then, after a disturbing e-mail from two people I had counseled with (before talking with this lady) concerning one dream in particular, I backed off for a time. They seemed to think a religious spirit was speaking through Elizabeth, so I quit praying for her dreams ... that is until we went to Pastor Benny Hinn's healing crusade in Atlanta. There he prayed that God would visit His people in their dreams, so I began praying once again for visitations by the Holy Spirit.

Elizabeth still wants me to pray for every little ache and pain she has and for her boo-boos to be healed. One night I was suffering with a serious attack of conjunctivitis in my left eye, and she got up on my bed to pray for me. She laid her little hand on my eye and said, "Devil, you get out of my mommy's eye right now!" Then she declared, "You're healed in Jesus' name," and it felt as if liquid fire was coming out of her hand. That was the end of her prayer, and my eye was completely healed the next morning!

TWO OF ELIZABETH'S DREAMS

January 16, 2005:

"I woke up and saw glowing angels all in my room. They were in the closet, and a glowing man was standing by my bed. [I asked Elizabeth if she knew who the man was, and she replied, 'Jesus.') I looked outside and our whole house was glowing. I got out of bed, and went downstairs to see where the glow was coming from. Our kitchen was full of angels. They were dancing, and singing and praising the Lord. One angel had on a sparkly robe with sparkling stars on it. The other angels had on gold robes and had gold-brown hair. They were on the stove, too. It was on, but they didn't get burned.

"A big angel that was almost as big as our house [we have a two story house] was in the middle of the kitchen. [She pointed to the place where our table is, and said the angel went up through the light fixture and roof. I believe she was seeing transparent angels, but didn't know the word for it.] I saw God, and He was so big He went up to the sky. Then I saw the devil and he was a little bitty man. [I had forgotten this part until she reminded me one day that God is bigger than 'the boogey man.']"

October 30, 2007:

"I was playing in the front yard, and decided to climb a tree. I saw Jesus and got down out of the tree. He started talking to me while we walked back to the house. He asked me if I knew what I was going to be when I grew up, and I told Him, 'No, not really.' He said, 'You are going to be a Holy Ghost Jesus Worship Leader.' He started teaching me Hebrew words. He taught me how to say cat, dog and hello in Hebrew. When we got to the front door, I rang the door bell, and when I turned around to say 'Bye,' He was gone."

SOME OF LAUREN'S DREAMS AND A VISION

June 30, 2007

A Vision: "I was in the basement rollerskating because it was raining outside. Something told me to go outside, so I got my umbrella and walked out the basement door. I saw a huge cloud that was parting with the sun coming out of the middle of it. It was in the West. [This is strange because it was already dusk.] I started thinking about the ten days of tribulation I overheard Mom talking about to one of her friends and wondered if that was a sign Jesus was coming back in the clouds."

The First Dream: "I was looking outside my bedroom window. It was facing West. I saw the same thing that I had seen in the vision, so I started trying to be really good and kept watching. I kept watching and waiting, never going to sleep. Suddenly it felt like something fell off me that was really heavy—sadness. I felt something else come on me—not perfectness or goodness. It was purity and it made me happy.
Suddenly I went into the next dream. We (Mom, Elizabeth and I) were standing on a cloud and I heard a trumpet. I said, 'Mom, close your eyes.' Then we were gone!"

February 28, 2008:

"I saw an Indian warrior come out of the house across the street from our house. He had long black hair and was wearing a cowboy bolo tie. He just looked around, but didn't say a word. When he went back in the house, a woman came out. She stood in front of our yard, in the street, and said, 'Ambassador, Ambassador.' She was a Russian woman. There were three kids behind her riding a bike. It only had one seat."

My Own Dreams

I've had several powerful dreams myself and have decided to share here the strangest one. It occurred just before dawn on April 6, 2007, Good Friday.

Somewhere around 2:30 AM, while I was waiting for the coffee to perk, I fell asleep and had a dream. In the dream I was driving my car, but was having difficulty seeing through the windshield. I tried the button that releases the window-washing solvent several times, but nothing came out.

Suddenly, I was moved to the passenger seat, and a man with black hair was behind the steering wheel. He never spoke, nor turned his head to look at me. I have always felt that he was an angel or maybe even the Lord Himself.

When I looked out the windshield now, I could see a huge fire that looked like it was coming up from one of the interchanges in Atlanta (like the one at Spaghetti Junction). Suddenly, we lifted above the expressway, and I saw devastation everywhere—railroad boxcars lying in pieces, tractor-trailers strewn all over the expressway and people walking around like they were in a daze, not saying a word. The fire was so vivid and huge, it looked like the earth opened up and the blazes were coming out of Hell.

I was so distraught when I woke up that I asked the Lord if that might have been a vision. (I've heard that when you see color in your dreams, it's usually a vision. The fire was the most vivid part of the dream, and I asked Him to please show me if it was a vision.)

Then, although I was wide awake, I felt a strong slumber come over me, and I fell asleep and dreamed again.

This time I was in a place I knew was a morgue. There were drawers as far as I could see that contained bodies, and I was looking for #4251. I awoke before I could find the body I was looking for. I felt it might possibly be confirmation of a huge disaster, or peril, destined for Atlanta in the future.

After pondering all of that for a few moments, I asked the Lord to show me if there was something else. Then I fell asleep again. This time I saw a huge transfer of wealth, and news came that oil had been found on ground owned by Native Americans.

DREAMS OF PURPOSE

In 2004, some very dear friends who live in Minnesota, Donna Ann Walling and Deb Reed, began going on spiritual journeys to Indian Reservations belonging to the Lakota Tribe. These women are some of the most anointed intercessors I've ever known. I shared a vision with Donna that I believe came from the Lord, in which natural resources would be revealed on the land they were going to pray over. On July 12th, Donna called to let me know that the Lord had told them to go back to South Dakota and pray over that land again. This time they would be going with a greater anointing that would bring the prophetic into reality. I reminded Donna of the vision about the resources, and I strongly believed one of them would be oil. Only time will tell if the dreams I had were visions that will come to pass.

I believe that sometimes God allows you to have a dream about a pending disaster so you can seek Him for mercy, praying against it actually happening or, at least, seeking protection for your loved ones through it. This is what He did for Abraham concerning Sodom and Gomorrah, and Lot was spared.

ELIZABETH WAS HEALED

During our regular church worship service on March 3, 2003 (03/03/03), I lifted Elizabeth up to the Lord and began praying for her in the Holy Ghost. Suddenly, He stopped me, and instructed me to tell her that her angels were before God, and for her to ask Jesus for her healing. As soon as Elizabeth asked Jesus to heal her, our pastor stopped the worship service and announced that God had just told him at least ten people needed to come forward.

I ran as fast as I could with Elizabeth in my arms, screaming, "Breaker! Breaker!" in my spirit. As soon as I put her into our pastor's arms, I began thanking Jesus for her healing. That night more than forty people were healed from asthma. Elizabeth discontinued her medications that night and has not had to go back to the doctor since for asthma treatments.

It was amazing to me that so many people were in our service who were suffering from asthma. It was as if there was a spiritual summons, a mandate from the master, to be there! Some of them had come with their oxygen tanks. Our pastor said he received calls, letters and e-mails from people for the next several days and weeks with doctors' reports confirming their healing.

I saw a revelation from that experience I've never forgotten: Your breaking point is the birth canal (breakthrough), to propel your burden from within your spirit to the natural, where it becomes your blessing. Extreme praise and worship fuels the breaker anointing, and it's available for all who are willing to seek it!

ANOTHER LIFE-CHANGING TRUTH

Another life-changing truth from Pastor Rod Parsley that has helped give me a bigger picture of this powerful weapon that is available to us is the revelation that God is a progressive God. In Isaiah 58 God talks about His chosen fast. It is *"to loose the bands of wickedness, to undo the heavy burdens, and to* let the oppressed go free, and that ye break every yoke" (Isaiah 58:6). In other words, His chosen fast is not about food; it's about deliverance. If God is a progressive God, then it's easier for us to break yokes than it is for us to "call the sabbath a delight" (Isaiah 58:13).

THE NAME DAVID

The most commonly occurring person's name in the Bible is David. It occurs one thousand eighty-five times. This is not a coincidence. David was referred to as "a man after [God's] own heart" (Acts 13:22). He was a warrior who praised God with his whole heart. It was David who said, "I will bless the LORD at all times: his praise shall continually be in my mouth" (Psalm 34:1). Is it any wonder, then, that he was the only person in the Bible said to be "after [God's] own heart." I believe one of the most important reasons God wants us to praise Him is so that He can inhabit our praises and thus fellowship with us. His Word declares: "But thou art holy, O thou that inhabitest the praises of Israel" (Psalm 22:3).

God is a holy God, and sin cannot stand in His presence. Thus the power and purpose behind the breaker anointing. Our praises that invite His presence will destroy every yoke!

WHY?

I asked the Holy Spirit to help me understand why it was so difficult for us to observe the Sabbath and call it a delight. It seemed as if that would be much easier than freeing the oppressed and breaking yokes. One thing that seemed to jump out at me in verse 13 was the wording: "and call the sabbath a delight, the holy of the LORD." The Sabbath is synonymous with rest, and holy means "to be set apart." The Bible says, "There *remaineth therefore a rest to the people of God. For he that is entered into his rest, he also hath ceased from his own works, as God did from his. Let us labour therefore to enter into that rest"* (Hebrews 4:9-11). Jesus warned that unbelief would keep us from entering that rest.

I recently heard it said, "When we work, God rests, and when we rest, God works." It's taken me a very long time to realize that no matter how much I want to see unsaved loved ones filled with the joy of the Lord and know how much they're loved by God, I can't make it happen—no matter how hard I work at it. So I've just set my heart on delighting myself in the Lord, knowing that His promise is to give me the desires of my heart (see Psalm 37:4).

My work has now shifted to my rest, as my faith continues to grow in the assurance that someday it will happen—in God's timing, not mine. Whether it happens on this side of Heaven or the other doesn't really matter to me!

ANOTHER EXCITING TREASURE

In addition to my praise and worship being a delight to God, I've found another exciting treasure in Proverbs 8: *"In the beginning of his way, before his works of old, ... or ever the earth was, ... I was by him, as one brought up with him: and I was daily his delight, rejoicing always before him"* (Proverbs 8:22-23 and 30). In that powerful chapter, wisdom declares: *"I love them that love me; and those that seek me early shall find me"* (Proverbs 8:17). Not only do I delight in the Lord, but my continual prayer is to become His delight daily!

Have you ever sought wisdom? Do you know where to find her? James tells us: *"If any of you lack wisdom, let him ask of God, that giveth to all men liberally.... But let him ask in faith, nothing wavering. For he that wavereth is like a wave of the sea driven with the wind and tossed"* (James 1:5-6).

Although I only had a brief moment in the Courtyard, the impact it made on my life continues even today. I pray that the Holy Spirit will stir every person reading this chapter to pursue praise with passion, knowing that it is God's whole-hearted desire to fellowship with us through our passionate praise.

It's time to accept *The Bride's Manifesto.*

CHAPTER 5

THE WAR ROOM

For unto us a child is born, unto us a son is given: and the government shall be upon his shoulder: and his name shall be called Wonderful, Counsellor, The mighty God, The everlasting Father, The Prince of Peace. Of the increase of his government and peace there shall be no end, upon the throne of David, and upon his kingdom, to order it, and to establish it with judgment and with justice from henceforth even for ever. The zeal of the Lord of hosts will perform this.

Isaiah 9:6-7

Somehow I sensed, during the last visitation to the Chamber of the Bridegroom, that these visits were about to end. So many things had happened during the past six weeks, things I simply couldn't explain in the natural. There was absolutely nothing perverted or sexual about any of the visits, yet they had carried my senses to a new level. No words were ever spoken by anyone; it seemed that I just sensed everything.

One of the most amazing phenomena occurred while I was dancing with Jesus, the Bridegroom. Although I never heard the music with my ears, I knew it was Davidic, as if I could see and feel the music without hearing it.

Visiting Another Area

As with the other few occasions that were spent outside the Chamber, I suddenly appeared in another area. It was a hallway that I sensed was in a government building with top-level security. I walked by a door that caught my immediate attention. "War Room" seemed to overtake my thoughts. Although there were no visible signs anywhere, things were being revealed to me instantly.

I began to cry out in my spirit for Jesus to do something so miraculous in my life that I might one day be allowed access to that room. My mind raced wildly, as I anticipated the very thought of being allowed to see war strategy that was being planned and implemented during the last days.

Now Things Made Sense

Things were beginning to make more sense to me now, as I reflected back on an article I had read by Jill Austin in January of 2000. She had written prophetic insights about the upcoming decade that stirred something so deep within my spirit that I couldn't shake it.

She talked about branches of the military in God's government and the role they would play in taking entire cities for Christ during the last days. I asked the Lord then, as I noted in a previous chapter, to please put me in boot camp and train me in all branches of His special forces. I was willing to start out as a foot soldier, but eventually I wanted assignments in His air force, with authority over the principalities and rulers that were reigning over my city and holding the people in captivity.

I knew I wasn't the only one with a passion to see Jesus ruling and reigning over Atlanta. There had to be others. During the last few times I had ministered to the homeless in Woodruff Park in 1991, the thought of having to leave them felt like someone plunging a jagged knife into my heart then twisting it. I asked the Lord to please bring me back there one day, but this time with an army. There were so many people there who were in captivity and desperately needed to be set free. When I felt that all-familiar, unexplainable peace settle over me, I knew it would happen—in His timing.

IMPACT FULTON INDUSTRIAL

Then I had the privilege of participating in an outreach in 2007 unlike any I had ever witnessed before. It sent my mind racing back to 1991, and I wondered if my prayer was finally being answered. Impact Fulton Industrial began with a burden God placed in the heart of a business owner. As he shared that burden with others—churches, schools, other outreach ministries and businesses—people began volunteering to help. It was an awesome sight to behold.

Before it was over, twenty-nine people were saved and gave their hearts to Jesus, and many others were delivered. Since that event, held on June 16, 2007, reports had been coming in daily about changes and miracles happening to those who attended the outreach.

Back in the Chamber

Just as quickly as I had found myself in the hallway, I suddenly appeared again in the Chamber, but now an overwhelming sorrow seemed to drench me. My heart felt like it was going to fly right out of my body, and my emotions suddenly felt like they were on a roller coaster. For the first time since I had gotten saved in 1983 I realized that the short time we spend on Earth will be our only opportunity for intimacy with Jesus, our heavenly Bridegroom. Once we get to Heaven, we'll have to share Him with everyone else!

I felt like all the tears I had shed up until that day were a mere bucketful, compared to the river my soul was now releasing. I didn't want to leave His presence. It was so precious and holy. I wanted time to stand still. I was caught between two worlds, one that I didn't want to leave, and one that I knew it wasn't yet time to leave.

When I finally left the Chamber that day, I looked down to find that I was wearing a beautiful wedding garment, but, for some reason, I couldn't move my feet. When I lifted the garment to try to discover the reason, I saw it immediately. Underneath that beautiful garment, I was wearing heavy combat boots!

Immediately I looked back at Jesus and, much to my amazement, He had also changed garments. Then I saw my Commander-in-Chief smiling. As I pondered, "Something very significant is on the horizon," I found myself instantly back in the natural, sitting in my living room again.

Not Natural Cloth

Those garments I had seen were not constructed of natural cloth, and I thought about the scripture in Isaiah: *"To appoint unto them that mourn in Zion, ...the garment of praise for the spirit of heaviness"* (Isaiah 61:3). Would these *"garments"* perhaps be considered new positions of authority or empowerment? Many thoughts have crossed my mind as to what they represented. Perhaps one day I'll know for sure.

The following year I had another encounter that caused quite a stir in my spirit. I felt like God was showing me so many things, but I kept sensing that they were all for an appointed time—a later time. If there's one thing I've learned about God in my walk with Him, it's that His Kingdom operates on His own time. We may be living in a microwavable, instantaneous society, but God's system is more like the old-fashioned crock pot variety. Every time I would find myself "in a stew" because I felt like He was moving too slowly, I would get a mental picture of myself in the crock pot. (Yes, God does want us to laugh. It's the very best medicine for the soul!)

THE BURDEN WAS INCREASING

The burden for my city was increasing again, and it was becoming more and more difficult to drive through Atlanta on my way to work without weeping. My sixty-mile-each-way commute to work carried me through five different counties, and it was amazing to me to feel a spiritual climate change the moment I crossed the perimeter and entered into the city. There was a heaviness that was almost paralyzing.

I noticed a sudden increase in that heaviness soon after Hurricane Katrina hit New Orleans, and many thousands of stranded residents of that devastated city sought refuge in Atlanta. It made a palpable difference.

In the fall of 2003, I felt like I was giving birth to a vision for revival I had been carrying for my city for some twenty years. One of the most significant and exciting moments during that season was another visit to the War Room.

ANOTHER VISIT TO THE WAR ROOM

The visitations to the Chamber of the Bridegroom primarily involved myself, Jesus and the Holy Spirit. This time I was observing others in a place that seemed familiar to me. Although I couldn't see with physical eyes, thoughts that were being transmitted became visual. Summits were being planned, and archangels were being appointed to stand guard at the doors of these summits, to prevent the enemy from hearing or seeing end-time strategy.

When I actually witnessed one of these summits, I saw familiar names on the list of participants. I was saddened and apparently a bit judgmental when I realized that a certain children's pastor, a favorite of mine, was not mentioned. Immediately I felt a spiritual hot coal hit my tongue. It frightened me so badly I fell to my knees in repentance. A gentle hand lifted me back up and said in a very stern, authoritative voice, "THIS IS WAR!" It was a voice I "saw" in the Spirit, the voice of an angel, and then I knew that this was the heavenly War Room!

GOD'S GLORY OVER THE CHURCHES

The very heartbeat of my vision was God's glorious presence covering our city. One night Lauren asked a very strange question while we were driving home from her ballet practice. She wanted to know what was in front of all the churches we were passing. Since I didn't see anything, I asked her to describe what she was seeing. She said it wasn't a color, but it looked like you'd taken a piece from the end of a cloud and placed it in front of the churches. She was amazed that I didn't see it, because it was so obvious to her.

I asked her if she could remember the first time she had seen this vision. Her answer shocked me because the day she indicated was exactly one year from the day she first "fell out" in the Spirit. She'd been listening to Freddy Hayler's "Song of Angels–This Is Your Day." After noticing that she was missing, I went in search of her and found her in the living room, passed out in the Spirit.

When she later staggered into the kitchen, I asked her where she'd been. Her response was simply, "In the glory" (as if I should have known). A few nights before she had been listening to Pastor Benny Hinn talk about the glory. She was curled up in a fetal position and wanted everyone to be quiet and listen. Eventually she fell asleep in that position. When Lauren later saw God's glory in front of each church we passed, I believe it was His time to reveal that His glory has gone before every single congregation where His Word is being preached.

NEW LEVELS OF PRAYER

For several weeks after my visitations to the Chamber of the Bridegroom, I went into extreme praise and worship and praying in the Holy Ghost while driving to and from work. When I began sensing strongholds in certain areas, I went into a warring level of prayer, wanting so badly to see revival in Metro Atlanta. God spoke to me through a prophet to stop that. He had not yet called me or equipped me for that type of prayer, and I was moving the angels assigned to protect me out of their positions.

In my eagerness for promotion in God's military, I had

learned another lesson the hard way. Each promotion catapults you deeper into enemy territory. Unless you know you've been given authority, you could become lunch for the enemy—if you try to take authority over a power that's outside of your spiritual jurisdiction. *"And the evil spirit answered and said, Jesus I know, and Paul I know; but who are ye? And the man in whom the evil spirit was leaped on them, and overcame them, and prevailed against them, so that they fled out of that house naked and wounded"* (Acts 19:15-16).

A Challenging Month

October seems to be a very challenging month for me. In October of 1989 and again in October of 2005, the Lord led me through doors of opportunity to participate in journeys that I'm still gaining insight from today.

I sensed at the beginning of October, 2005, from the on-slaught of adversity coming against me, that I was being considered for promotion. Then, the first Sunday morning in that month something picked me up and slammed me to the floor in Kid's Church in front of two of our elders. I was just bending over to tie a scroll Elizabeth had in her hand, and this "thing" flipped me over and knocked me to the floor. It felt like my skull and tailbone were fractured.

I tried to make a joke out of what had happened because I didn't want to cause fear in the children. "I thought I left that thing outside when I came in," I joked. One of the elders laughed, but then he said that he'd been having some crazy experiences too.

The following evening, while I was sitting at our kitchen table talking to my son Ray, something felt like it smashed into my left shin. By Wednesday I was in so much pain I had to go to a doctor. After examining an x-ray of the affected area, he said, "I don't know what you did, but you have the shin splints from Hell." We really had a good laugh over that one. I already knew where they'd come from. He didn't have to tell me.

He put a walking cast on me, and that presented a real challenge when one of the journeys I was led to take that month was to Dog River. In the end, we had to change the actual place our prayer team was planning to pray over, because the cast put limits on my ability to walk over rugged terrain. After arriving at our revised location, however, we knew that was where God had intended for us to be all along.

That same week I reached behind the French doors in my bedroom to turn the light off, and something slammed me into the door. My body weight smashed into my right wrist so hard that it nearly broke. I woke up Wednesday morning with a bruise on my forehead that I hadn't had when I went to bed. I couldn't help but laugh when I noticed that it was off-center. I reminded the enemy that none of his weapons were going to prosper and taunted him with the thought that he was such a poor shot he couldn't even hit a bull's eye squarely!

I was cooking Tuesday afternoon of that same week, and as Ray turned to walk away from the sink, a spider suddenly appeared out of nowhere. It was crawling down a string-like web from the ceiling. He killed it and then decided to examine it, suspecting that it might be a brown recluse (a very dangerous poisonous spider, for those who might not know). Sure enough, it was a recluse.

I had been bitten twice, ten days apart, by brown recluse spiders a couple of years prior to that. The surgeon who treated the bite on my finger was amazed that I didn't lose it. The other bite was on my face. When that one came, I had been through so much Hell with the first bite that I wasn't about to let the enemy do a repeat, so I launched my own counterattack on Hell. The result was that I didn't even have to go to the doctor with that second bite.

In spite of all the weapons the enemy tried to use against me that October, none of them prospered. He didn't even get a toehold of fear on me. The three journeys I went on that year were parallels with the journeys I had gone on in 1989.

THE THREE JOURNEYS OF 1989

Even though I was still in a denominational church in 1989, I sensed that God was showing me something about deliverance. He opened a door that month for me to visit a young man who was in solitary confinement in our local jail. A family acquaintance had gotten locked up for domestic problems and was serving his time as a trustee. He told me that he felt sorry for this man because other trustees were planning to do something bad to him.

The young man had asked him for a Bible, and so I sent word for him to put my name on his visitors' list, as a visitor from our church. As a result, I was able to lead that young man to Christ just a week before he was to be sentenced to life imprisonment plus twenty years, for kidnapping and setting fire to his girlfriend (he was high on heroine when he did it).

A week later I went on another journey where the Lord showed me the power of binding and loosing prayers in a miracle at a sports event that made national headlines. I hadn't wanted to go back to that particular area because when I had been there two years earlier, I had seen an evil work in the Spirit against children. I begged God all week to provide me with a way of escape, but there was no answer. The morning I had to leave, I had a very painful cluster headache, and by the time I arrived at the place, I felt like I was close to death.

While someone went to get me some medication for my headache, I asked God for a miracle that would be so humiliating it would destroy the evil work I sensed. When He answered, "I will; start praying," I seemed to move into a level of grace that lifted me above the pain. For thee and a half hours I prayed the binding and loosing prayers and witnessed supernatural things happening right before my eyes. That was my first experience with commissioning angels to specific assignments (and I was still in a church where we didn't hear about things like this happening).

After the event was over, I wept while those around me were celebrating *their* victory. I felt like I was the only one who knew what had really happened that day. The real victory was all about the enemy's assignments being broken.

WHAT DID IT ALL MEAN?

I began thinking about revival and the power of those prayers I had just prayed. I asked God to please send me a woman who would be willing to take on the hoards of Hell and believe in the power of those kinds of prayers. I believed that together we could help start revival.

Although the binding and loosing prayers I prayed had been effective in that particular incident, I'm grateful for an even greater understanding the Lord has now given me through the books of Liberty Savard. Her trilogy (*Shattering Your Strongholds: Freedom from Your Struggles* [Gainsville, Florida; Bridge-Logos: 1992], *Breaking the Power: Of Unmet Needs, Unhealed Hurts, Unresolved Issues in Your Life* [Gainsville, Florida; Bridge-Logos: 1997] and *Producing the Promise: Keys of the Kingdom* [Gainsville, Florida; Bridge-Logos: 1999]) has helped me gain a much better understanding of another powerful enemy—my own unsurrendered soul, and her training-wheel prayers have been so priceless in my walk with the Lord that I keep her books next to my Bible.

If you feel like you've been taking baby steps lately, the revelation you will find in these books will help you take quantum leaps. This is one of the best investments you could ever make—if you desire to walk in the fullness of your destiny.

THE FINAL JOURNEY

The final journey in October of 1989 was a spiritual one. I had read *Satan's Underground: The Extraordinary Story of One Woman's Escape* (Stratford, Lauren; Gretna, Louisiana; Pelican Publishing Co.: 1991), and that book turned me inside out. I talked to ladies at our church and at work about helping me pray for God to turn the tables on Satan that Halloween. Some ladies were planning to keep their lights off that year, and I convinced some of them to keep them on. I asked them to put "Jesus pencils" and other items they could find at the Christian bookstores inside goody bags with candy for the children who would be coming by. Some of us fasted and prayed that week for miracles.

On Halloween morning, I had a wild experience while driving on I-20 East enroute to work. As I was pouring my heart out to God, using binding and loosing prayers against assignments I knew the enemy was planning for that night, a huge box fell off of a truck in front of me. I screamed, "Jesus!" and closed my eyes for a split second. When I opened them again, my car was being transported to the next lane. That was the first of many encounters I began having with angels!

NEARLY HIT AGAIN

Another such experience happened one morning when I

had begun praying those same prayers for my loved ones. I was crossing some railroad tracks, when a truck almost hit me head-on. As I swerved to avoid him, my right front tire went off the pavement and into a dropoff. I tried desperately to get my car out, but nothing worked. A lady stopped to see if I wanted her to call for help. Without thinking, I blurted out, "I don't have time! A train's coming."

There was no train in sight, but somehow I knew one was on the way. A man in a car behind me got out to help. He was very small in stature, so I silently prayed, "Jesus, please send an angel to help him." He told me to give the car some gas, while he tried lifting the side that was stuck. The result was that this little man picked my car up like it was a toy and sat it back on the pavement. As I ran back across the tracks to thank him, I looked up and saw the train coming!

ANOTHER ENCOUNTER

Several months later, I was exiting I-85 at Jimmy Carter Boulevard one morning on the way to work, when I saw a stalled car in the roadway. As I started to pray for help to come for the driver, the Holy Spirit said to me, "Stop!" So I pulled over.

A young woman was panicking because her gear shift lever was stuck. I began praying in the Holy Ghost for help because she was at one of the busiest exits on the expressway. A tractor trailer stopped behind my car, and the driver ran past me smiling, saying, "Stop the traffic!" Instantly, I knew I had seen that little man before. Where was it?

I held my hands out in front of me and prayed fervently in the Holy Ghost, and as I was praying, I remembered where I had seen him—on the railroad tracks that day! I sensed then that he was an angel.

As long as I held my hands out that day in prayer, not one car came off of I-85 onto that exit. Then, when I looked back and saw that the young woman's car had been moved to the shoulder of the road, I put my hands down, and suddenly it seemed like a dam had broken loose, and there was an onslaught of vehicles hitting that exit ramp. I had to literally run to my car to get out of their way.

Although I haven't seen my friend since then, I still believe he's somewhere around, waiting for another 911 call!

THE DOG RIVER TRIP

The journey I made to Dog River that October was an experience unlike anything I had ever participated in before. For several months prior to that, I had felt like there was a river I needed to go and pray over. My special friend, Donna, told me that the Holy Spirit had revealed to her in prayer that someone needed to pray over Dog River. There had been, He told her, a massacre on the banks of that river many years before.

For several weeks I kept seeing the impression in my spirit: "something old, something new, something borrowed, something blue." I knew that sounded like it represented wedding memorabilia, so I sensed this journey would have something to do with a wedding.

The morning we were getting ready to leave I found out from my former pastor, who had been praying for our journey, that he had also been drawn to the history of that river when he pastored a church in the area.

The river was named Dog River because of its twisted shape, like that of a dog's hind leg. I must admit, however, that I was drawn to the river because its name spelled God backward. I was sure that was significant.

There were four of us who went to the river. My daughter Lauren was a last-minute addition. It was a very emotional trip for all of us, with very little talking, just a lot of praying and worshiping. "A solemn assembly" is the best way I could describe the atmosphere that morning.

When we got to the river, there were visible signs confirming that we were exactly where God had intended us to be. As we stood in a circle at the edge of the water, holding hands, we began to weep and worship in prayerful repentance for what had happened during the massacre and in thanksgiving for what God was now doing. And we waited for the Holy Spirit to move.

None of us felt worthy to be there. It was very humbling, and we all felt that we were on Holy ground.

Lauren heard singing while we were praying, and another participant saw multitudes being fed by the river. We walked around the area at the edge of the river, and I prayed over the places where the soles of our feet were treading. I then stood on a rock, where I saw the Gospel being preached during the Tribulation. As we sang softly, I began prophesying over the rocks to "cry out supernaturally with songs of worship to God."

I walked upstream, to where I could step out onto the rocks. Not far from that area, Dog River dumps into the Chattahoochee. There I poured some water Donna had sent me from the headwaters of the Mississippi into the rushing white waters of the Dog River.

There was such a reverence and holiness in that place that I didn't want to leave. It was hard for all of us to walk away that day.

Each one of us sensed that one day (and I don't believe it will be long now) there would be another great massacre taking place on the banks of that river. I believe this will be one of the sites for the gathering of a Stephen company, those who will refuse to receive the mark of the beast and, instead, submit to death. I called forth spiritual children that day who would sit at the Master's table during the wedding feast. Although I knew there was great sorrow for those who would have to give their lives for the Gospel's sake, there was great joy over their salvation.

Unusual Acts

We did some things that morning with items we had taken with us, under the direction of the Holy Spirit, that I feel are too sacred to reveal at this time. All I can say is that the prophetic significance of every item we took on that journey was revealed and confirmed by other prophets, and everything pertained to a wedding.

Donna told me she had learned somewhere that the name Mississippi meant "River of the Holy Spirit." While I was pouring the water from the Mississippi into Dog River, I saw a beautiful picture of unity, as the river of God and the river of the Holy Spirit joined together.

I Love God's Analogies

I love God's analogies. The Holy Spirit showed me a beautiful picture of time and the Alpha and Omega that day at Dog River. It's like a superhighway or expressway. The right side is symbolic of your present, and the left side is symbolic of your past. The interesting thing is that you can never see the end of your present nor the beginning of your past. You're always aware of your past, but if you keep glancing over your shoulder or looking in your rearview mirror long enough, you will prematurely exit your present.

I believe your destiny involves your past and present journey, and there are many signs along the highway of life giving you directions. Yes, there are times when you need to stop and rest, but we're all on a journey to a great city.

Often you will see someone who is stranded or wounded along the way because of something others have done to them, and your assignment to them may be that of the Good Samaritan. We don't have to carry such people with us the entire journey, but we must pour into them whatever they need and take them to a safe place before we continue on our own way. Perhaps you've been the one someone else stopped to help, and now it's your turn to repay that act of mercy and kindness by helping others.

ENJOY THE DRIVE

On your own journey, enjoy the drive, for it's your destiny, not your destination. Keep the pathway clean for those who will follow you. Obey the speed limits. Don't wish your present life away by trying to get ahead of God. Keep the junk out of your trunk, and limit your own baggage so that you'll have room for the treasures He has to give you along the way.

Remember, you're not walking down this superhighway of life. You have a vehicle that's carrying you, and it's the Holy Spirit. If you will listen to His promptings, He will let you know when you're running out of gas or need more water in your radiator, or perhaps when it's time to let your engine cool down a bit.

Whatever you do, avoid road rage. It's a snare from the enemy to shorten your trip and take you out of your destiny prematurely and permanently.

ARE YOU SERIOUS?

For those of you who are serious about God's military, He

has assignments for you in every branch and on every level. As it was in the beginning, when Jesus left instructions for the Church, so it will be as it gets closer to His return for His Bride. She must be ready, whatever the cost. *"Many are called, but few are chosen"* (Matthew 22:14) for His special forces.

Again, there's a cost for the anointing. It will cost you everything, but it will pay what money can't afford to buy— precious souls for the Kingdom!

Whether you are walking in God's will or your own, there's a certainty that you will suffer adversity in this world. Life's not a bed of roses for anyone. Why not volunteer as a soldier in God's great army and start receiving His benefits for you and your family? If you can't do anything but pray, that's a position available to everyone—even small children—and it's always open-enrollment season.

So, get involved! Don't waste your opportunity to help us all make a difference for the Kingdom.

It's time to accept *The Bride's Manifesto.*

CHAPTER 6

UNITY THROUGH DIVERSITY

I therefore, the prisoner of the Lord, beseech you that ye walk worthy of the vocation wherewith ye are called.
Till we all come in the unity of the faith, and of the knowledge of the Son of God, unto a perfect man, unto the measure of the stature of the fulness of Christ.

Ephesians 4:1 and 13

A year after the season of powerful visitations in the Chamber of the Bridegroom, I found myself yearning for an even greater revelation of Christ's death, burial and resurrection, and I fervently sought another visit to the cross. This time, I felt a greater remorse for my own sin, as if I were the one who should have been on the cross—not Jesus!

Yes, I know that Jesus died for all my sins—past, present and future—and I realize that this is a very controversial subject with some Christians, but I don't believe that a religious spirit was controlling me during this season.

AN EXTREMIST FOR CHRIST

Mary Magdalene was rebuked for her extreme acts of devotion to Jesus after He had changed her life, and I find that the terrible tormenting fear I endured for so many years of my life (until Jesus delivered me) has also made me an extremist for Him. My gratitude for His amazing grace, that not only saved me from an eternal Hell, but also delivered my mind from a now-tormenting Hell, is something that mere words cannot express. I constantly look for opportunities to express, through actions, what my mouth is incapable of expressing through words.

I can relate, to an extent, with both Mary Magdalene and Mary of Bethany and what they suffered. Religious critics have not changed much in the past two thousand years. Their thoughtless words are still just as cutting as ever.

One of the reasons, I believe, these two women touched the heart of the Master was the genuineness of their tears. The rivers of tears that flowed from them, I am convinced, were not just in gratitude for the Master's love, acceptance and forgiveness. Those tears also flowed because of the pain inflicted on these women by others. And because of that, they knew a level of compassion that many never know. Unless a rose is crushed, you can only see the outward beauty of it. A crushed rose releases what's hidden, a fragrance so potent that it quickly fills a room with its presence.

Most Christians take their salvation far too lightly. We're not walking it out daily *"with fear and trembling"* as we should (Philippians 2:12). We've gotten so far from the reality of the cross that we're no longer shocked when we hear of someone who's been molested or murdered. Lives are being shattered by divorce and family violence, and we don't even seem to care. Indifference, to Jesus, is a putrid thing, and yet it continues to manifest through the ostrich syndrome in so many of us Christians, as we choose to ignore the needs in our own churches and communities.

I personally stand guilty as charged, for I can see the times I've been "too busy" to help others around me, and I'm asking God for wisdom and discernment now in rearranging my priorities to be of more service to those in need. The law of Christ is to bear one another's burdens: *"Bear ye one another's burdens, and so fulfil the law of Christ"* (Galatians 6:2).

MY CONTINUED PURSUIT OF THE CROSS

As I began my pursuit of the cross once again, I used one of the hassocks in my living room for a physical altar, and there I knelt to pour out my heart to God. I envisioned four horns on the hassock (one on each corner), and laid myself on the altar of sacrifice, praying for the fire of God to consume every ounce of my flesh, so that I could learn how to dwell in His glorious manifest presence.

This experience brought to my remembrance another journey that occurred during 1992, a time when I asked God to break my will until it was in total submission to His own for my life. The Holy Spirit gently revealed to me that I was on the way to my Gethsemane. Although I was frightened at the thought of what might happen, I knew I must press on. The door had recently closed for me in a denominational church, where I had been part of a ladies' evangelism program for eight years.

I had seen more people saved in 1991 than I had seen in the seven years prior to that. I'm not talking about people just repeating a prayer; I'm talking about something powerful hitting them. I had connected to a power source that many didn't seem to understand.

The book of Acts had "messed me up," and I kept praying for the power Peter had received at Pentecost to fall on me too. I reminded God that He was no respecter of persons, and whatever He did for Peter I wanted Him to do for me. The result was that miracle after miracle began happening. And still I wasn't satisfied. I wanted more!

I Didn't Let Fear Stop Me

Some were frightened at what was happening to me, but I didn't let their fear stop me. When I began to get extremely radical with my prayers, my whole life turned upside down. My job was suddenly phased out at the company I was working for, and I was placed in a severely difficult financial position.

Although friends at church kept assuring me that God would intervene and not allow me to lose my home, I sensed deep down inside my being that He was not punishing me. He was up to something good!

Although it took several months for the process to play out, the home was lost, and I began to pray for discernment about where I should live and work. It was then that a door opened for a job at the company I presently work for, and I was able to rent an apartment two miles from the office.

During that period I poured myself into the Word of God and began asking Him to break my will. I found a scripture about the early rain and latter rain that stirred so much passion within me that I began reflecting on some of the miracles that God had done in my life. If that was the *"early"* rain, then what would the *"latter"* rain be like? Although I looked at every ministry experience—especially salvation—as a miracle, there were three that are forever embedded in the chambers of my heart.

I saw the full spectrum of God's unconditional love cover the "up-and-outer," as well as the "down-and-outer!"

DEALING WITH DISAPPOINTMENTS

After a very disappointing moment, when I was so sure God was going to touch loved ones' hearts during a revival at our church, my heart was crushed. I had fasted and prayed so fervently, even having other friends praying for God to speak through the visiting evangelist, but those who needed it seemed indifferent to his powerful messages.

The next morning I asked God if He would please put someone of authority in my path to minister to, perhaps one of my bosses. I had to know that He had not left me because I was feeling so discouraged and powerless in my prayer life. That very morning a door opened for me to work with a world-renowned international financial consultant. Our landlord's secretary was sick, so I was chosen from all the other secretaries in our business complex to work with this man for three days.

I love God's sense of humor. I had not taken any clerical or secretarial courses in high school, not even typing, because I had been planning to go on to college. But when my foster mother suddenly died, those plans fell by the wayside.

After entering the public workplace, I quickly realized that Latin and Algebra weren't going to help me much. I needed miracles! The Lord has richly blessed me with doors of opportunity that He has opened for the past forty-five years. I've been in positions that I was not formally trained for and excelled in each position. My present salary exceeds that of most college graduates, so I can look back over my life and see how He honored my pleas for miracles (and my hard work)! Now I had this new opportunity.

I prayed constantly, as I worked with this brilliant man, who had been a professor at both Harvard and Yale. To me, it was simply beyond words that God would do this for me. As the final day of my service to the man approached, I began seeking the Lord for wisdom, and a door to open for me to minister to him. And did it ever!

The words the Lord gave me for the man were so powerful that they shocked both of us. I almost went to my knees because I couldn't even bring myself to look at him. It was a warning that shook my very foundation. It was somewhat of a frightening experience because I knew it wasn't me speaking.

The man gently put his hand on my shoulder and looked into my teary eyes, and I will never forget the last words he spoke to me: "You're a remarkable woman. Don't ever stop what you're doing." I began praying for him afterwards because I knew he would go through more storms and fires than he had ever faced in his life. Although we never met again, I prayed for him for several years.

Another Painful Period

During another painful season in my life, I felt I had to move in with my youngest son and his wife. Again I asked God to do something special in my life, to help ease the pain I was feeling. This time, He worked, through a very bizarre set of circumstances, to put a woman and her business manager in my path. They were staying at the Peachtree Plaza during a visit to the Atlanta Merchandise Mart.

After finishing a special ministry assignment that I had been praying for, I was getting ready to leave our church's rescue mission in Atlanta. It had been a desire of mine for several months to help serve food to the homeless, and doing so had proven to be such a joy for me.

After helping with the clean-up, I was anxious to leave the mission before dark. Then a young man from Puerto Rico asked if he could tell me his testimony, and I felt honored that he wanted to share it with me. He had just finished his testimony when someone put a phone in my hand, saying that the call was for me.

The man on the line asked if someone from our church could pick him and his business associate up the following day and take them to our Sunday morning church service. I had no idea who they were, but I said I would be glad to come and take them.

The drive from their hotel to the church took about thirty minutes, so the lady and I had a very nice chat on the way. She seemed very interested in my personal situation and was astounded that I still had so much joy in the midst of it.

Later, sitting in the ladies Sunday school classroom, she began telling me about her own situation. Her husband was a very influential and prosperous attorney, but he couldn't handle her success. Her product line was very popular during the 1980s and had made her very wealthy. When he eventually asked her for a divorce, she was crushed.

When she asked me how I was able to handle my own situation with so much joy, the door opened for me to tell her about Jesus. Through tears, but with great hope, she listened to the words the Lord had for her, and then she accepted Him as her Savior. Later, her manager told me that he and his wife had been fasting and praying for her salvation. They stepped out in faith believing that if he could get her to Atlanta, she would be saved. And she was!

The Coldest Night of the Year

One cold Friday night in February, 1991, I began weeping as I listened to the evening news. It was going to be the coldest night so far that winter, and there was great concern for the homeless who might not be able to find shelter. I cried and prayed myself to sleep that night. At 3:00 AM that next morning I was awakened, and I went into the living room and began reading my Bible. After a few minutes, I got on my face and began praying because I sensed that someone in Atlanta was near death.

For two hours, I prayed and called down angels. I envisioned places in Atlanta where I commissioned them to go and protect those who might be outside in the bitter cold. After feeling a release, I got up and dressed. It didn't matter whether anyone else in our evangelism group went to Atlanta that morning or not. I was determined to go.

I had a battle persuading our pastor's mother to go into Atlanta with me, but in the end she agreed, primarily because she didn't want me to go alone. I was adamant about going to Woodruff Park, for I just knew I was going to find the one I'd been praying for!

Temperatures had plunged into the single digits during the night, and it was still extremely cold in the park, even though the sun was peeking between the skyscrapers. The two of us had on boots, long wool coats, gloves and scarves, and still the wind sent a chill through our clothing that made us feel like we were dressed for summer. Shortly before 10:30 AM that morning, I found the person I was seeking.

Ted Tucker had arrived in Atlanta during the night, and had been forced to sleep in a parking lot because all the shelters were full. He had come from a warm climate, so he was wearing only a light jacket. Someone had given him a thin blanket, and that was the only protective clothing he'd had to help him survive the bitter cold, as he tried to sleep on the concrete pavement. When I began telling Ted about being awakened to pray, tears began flowing down his cheeks. In that moment, he started to realize what a miracle it was that he had survived the night, and just how important he was to God. He was so important that God had awakened me and sent me more than twenty miles, seven hours later, to express that love to him.

After listening to the words the Lord had for him, Ted accepted Jesus as his Savior. I told him not to ever forget just how much God loved him, no matter how bad things might get in the future.

Many More Miracles

Although there were many more miracles and ministry experiences that happened during the late 1980s and early 1990s, something kept stirring inside me, as I thought about the latter rain. If we were experiencing such power way back then, just what did *the future* hold? It was that anticipation deep within my very being that kept driving me closer to the garden.

I still remember the moment I looked into the cup of sorrows, as if it were yesterday.

The Journey to Golgotha

Although it had now been so long ago since that journey to the garden, I felt as if it had just happened, and the cross was next. As I reflected more and more on the events leading up to the crucifixion, I thought about the journey to Golgotha. Soon I began to understand why it was so important for Simon, a Cyrenian, to take up Christ's cross and bear it for Him. Now that's what *He* does for us, whenever our burdens become too heavy for us to bear. Whenever we lay them at His feet, He instantly picks them up.

That's why the Lord's promise to never leave nor forsake us is so powerful. No matter how painful our journey becomes on the highway of life, He's there with us—every step of the way—to meet whatever need we might have!

The more I walk with the Lord, the more convinced I am that everything begins and ends with the cross. It was there I realized that no amount of fancy clothing could hide my sins, so I willingly laid aside my own righteousness. This journey is futile, unless you're willing to come clean and strip yourself of your own filthy rags of self-righteousness. There is no hiding place at the cross for sin. It's fully exposed in all its ugliness! You must have a desire to become so transparent that even flesh can't find a place to hide. Unless you're willing to be judged at the feet of Christ on Earth, at the cross, you'll be judged at the seat of Christ in Heaven!

A Root of Bitterness

Roots of bitterness can harden the kindest hearts. The Bible warns us to beware of offences, for they *will* come, but it's what we do with the offences that affects our hearts. Words *do* hurt, especially if they're hurled by someone we love very deeply. But God's mercy is everlasting, and He expects us to freely give to others what He has freely given unto us.

Because of the very nature of the crucifixion, God will not excuse nor condone unforgiveness in us. Jesus died for the sins of mankind, and the work was finished at the cross. In turn, we're to pick up our cross and follow Him. In the process, however, we're to put down our offences. Jesus will deal with those offenders. He said, *"Woe unto the world because of offences! for it must needs be that offences come; but woe to that man by whom the offence cometh!"* (Matthew 18:7).

Spiritual Sickness

Although I've suffered from many illnesses and afflictions in the natural, I didn't realize just how devastating the spiritual counterparts were until I willing gave Jesus the cat-of-nine-tails and allowed myself to identify with His stripes. Spiritual autism, spiritual heart disease and spiritual arthritis were three of the most deadly. May God deliver us from these evils!

Thousands suffer from different forms of arthritis. When it happens to you, there's so much stiffness and pain in your body that you ache every time you move. I can speak about this from experience. It's *very* painful. I sensed that a lot of Christians suffer from spiritual arthritis because of their rebellion (stiffneckedness), and they end up in a dry place. Jesus is the water of life, and your daily walk with Him will keep you full of joy, and your joints "well-lubed!"

Doctors who treat rheumatoid diseases warn their patients about becoming immobile. Walking is the number one choice for good exercise. We need to walk with Jesus!

I've heard that the thirty-nine stripes Jesus bore for our healing represented thirty-nine diseases that plague mankind. I wonder if it's possible that there's a key to understanding the spiritual counterparts, especially with generational diseases. This could unleash a wave of healing when iniquities (the sins of our forefathers) are confessed and washed away by the cleansing blood of Jesus. It's something to think about!

Dying to Self

During this time, even though I was a woman and didn't have a beard, I asked the Lord to rip off the façade that I'd hidden behind for so long. Years of rejection had caused me to mask the real me as a defensive tactic, to shield myself from hurtful people. I had gotten so used to hiding my own identity that it wasn't that difficult to ask Him to mar my own visage, so that nothing remained of the old self. I wanted something new to be resurrected. I was ready for a spiritual facelift!

I believe this conscious decision to lose my life that I might find it was exactly what Christ commanded all of us to do. Until there is death to self, you can't experience the resurrected life. You can die to self by your willingness to give everything up—life, reputation, family, vision, etc. No matter how pretty my talk is, if I'm not "walking" my talk, the world only sees a hypocrite walking with empty, hollow, powerless eyes and a powerless testimony!

Nailed to the Cross

One of the most amazing revelations came when I gave the Lord the nails and asked Him to nail my feet and hands to the cross. As the nails pierced nerves, muscles and tendons, I envisioned the old life completely draining out, as the blood flowed from them. Two feet, once divided, were now *"fitly joined together."* They would leave the cross walking in dominion and destiny, remaining joined in unity through diversity in my spiritual walk.

This was a picture of my total dependence on the Holy Spirit for His guidance in the steps that had been ordered by God. Faith legs would be strengthened, as balance was obtained through daily workouts, with the threefold cords that served as spiritual umbilical cords and kept me connected to my source of nourishment and strength (see Romans 14:17, Proverbs 2:6, and 1 Corinthians 13:13).

MY HANDS TOO

For each hand nailed to the cross, there were five divided fingers, each representing specific sins I'd been guilty of. My spiritual right hand of fellowship should have been in control, but my fleshly left hand seemed to take control more often, causing my walk and talk to be out of balance. As these hands (actually wrists) were pierced with nails, those nails severed nerves, muscles and tendons. Fingers became limp as the life flowed out, with the blood.

The left thumb represented my will; the right represented God's will. The left forefinger represented the one pointed in judgment toward others; the right one pointed back at me, as I judged myself according to the righteousness of Christ.

The left middle finger represented offences; while the one on the right represented unconditional love, acceptance and forgiveness. The third finger on the left hand is the ring finger, which represents marriage and covenant relationship in the natural. The third finger on the right hand represents the new covenant, where the spiritual ring has already been placed, making me a third-day bride, one who is keeping herself ready for the Bridegroom when He comes to take her to the marriage feast.

The smallest finger on the left hand is the finger of control (through the Jezebel spirit). It's also a picture of subtle deception when someone twists, or coils, you around their little finger. That's exactly what the serpent did to Eve, and Samson lost his anointing because of Delilah's little finger. That little finger brought death to each one!

The right little finger, when surrendered to the Holy Spirit, can manifest spiritual strength, through faith, that is incomprehensible. Think of the "pinkie promises" that kids make. They are unbreakable! God's "pinkie promises" are always yes and amen!

After the blood was drained from each finger, and those lifeless appendages became fitly joined together, they formed hands outstretched to lost and dying souls standing on the edge of eternity.

When you tuck your thumb into the palm of your hand (a picture of submitting your will) and hold the hand up, it looks like an arrowhead. The two longest appendages on each hand, fitly joined together in unity and perfect harmony, represent the unconditional love, acceptance and forgiveness of Almighty God that will impact the Kingdom!

THE TESTIMONY OF THE CRUCIFIED DISCIPLE

I believe the Holy Spirit showed me another picture of what Jesus meant when He said that we would do greater works than He did, because He went back to the Father. The crucified disciple's testimony will reach out, so endued with power, that both thieves will be snatched from Hell's handbag.

Satan sent two liars to give false testimony that found Jesus guilty and led to His arrest and crucifixion, but it's payday for the one who tempted Eve with forbidden fruit. He's about to lose twice as much! The true testimony of the crucified disciple will reap twice the harvest of souls for Jesus when he or she declares them forgiven and rewards them with eternal life.

Just the moment the enemy thinks he's about to populate Hell, the dead, buried and resurrected disciple will exercise his authority given by Christ, as He releases the anointing that destroys the yokes. They will then be raptured right out of the enemy's hands. In the twinkling of an eye, their eternal destination will be changed—right before Satan's very eyes!

THE CROWN OF THORNS

When I asked Christ to place the crown of thorns on my head, I saw blood streaming from my mind, depleting it of all traces of life in the natural realm. I wanted holy amnesia so that I would have His renewed mind, void of the remembrance of sin! Some of my biggest headaches occurred when I got too close to curiosity about the fall and the enemy. It was better, I found, not to know too much. I believe we are on a journey back to the original garden, where minds are only filled as commanded by Paul in Philippians: *"Whatsoever things are true, ... honest, ... just, ... pure, ... lovely, ...of good report; ... if there be any praise, think on these things"* (Philippians 4:8). A new day is dawning, an awakening to innocence and purity that began in the Garden.

FROM THE PIERCED SIDE

As for Jesus' side, it was the hands of a sinner piercing Him that symbolically gave birth to His Bride, the Church. The disciples were fully empowered at Pentecost and worked closely with their helpmeet, the Holy Spirit, to establish the Church. Later, when religious traditions crept into the church, it fell asleep, and the enemy took control. The wedding garments became soiled and wrinkled. It's past time for us to take back the Church of the living Christ and establish His Kingdom on Earth as it is in Heaven. The hour is now for the crucified disciple to be resurrected and become Christ's glorious Bride, without spot or wrinkle!

103

From the crucified disciple's side, I saw Christ, with the sword, piercing him or her for the birthing of the end-time radical remnant warriors, who would usher in His glorious return, a picture of multiplication! These will come forth fully empowered to bring everything, all of creation, full circle, back to God, and restore the Garden of Eden. Their helpmeet is also the Holy Spirit. Just as Eve was created from Adam's side, as a fully mature woman who was ready to be Adam's bride, so will the radical remnant be fully matured and ready to march as the unified Bride of Christ.

SOMETHING ELSE POWERFUL TO THINK ABOUT

Here's something else powerful to think about: Jesus was able to remit people's sins even before He died on Calvary. Why do you suppose He was able to walk in that authority? He knew that He had been given that authority by God through sonship, and His miracles testified of that authority. Even though He was the literal Son of God, He did not leave Heaven operating in that authority. Sonship was revealed to Him as He matured: *"And the child grew, and waxed strong in spirit, filled with wisdom: and the grace of God was upon him"* (Luke 2:40).

As born-again Christians, we have been given the same sonship authority as Christ operated in, and miracles will follow all those who walk and operate in that authority! We must, however, follow in His footsteps, growing in our relationship with Him, becoming strong in spirit, being filled with wisdom and walking in grace. This is a progressive walk, one that keeps gaining power, and it's also corporate, that is it requires the entire Body of Christ, not just one member, to fulfill the mandate left to the Church! Could it be that this revelation of our Sonship authority is one of the keys to the latter rain?

THE BEGINNING OF THE LATTER RAIN?

The Breaker has gone before us, and we're already seeing so many miracles that I personally believe we're now experiencing the beginning of the latter rain. In the garden, God told Adam to subdue and have dominion over every living thing that moved upon the face of the earth. If we're subduing and walking in dominion, then we're taking the very presence of God (Peter's "shadow") wherever we go, and Satan is exposed the minute he tries to show up. He can't hide in the Shekinah glory.

We've come full circle. We've been reconciled back to God. Everything has been restored to its original state, as if sin had never existed! I believe God is anxious for us to catch this revelation and begin operating in it, so He can, once again, walk with us in the cool of the day!

MAJOR BACK SURGERY

In 1988, I had to have major back surgery. A beating I suffered in 1974 at the hands of a woman recently released from a mental hospital had left me with me a broken vertebra in the thoracic area of my spine and five herniated discs. My neck whipped so violently that after the fifth whiplash, doctors told me that if it whipped again, more than likely, my neck would break. On Friday, May 13, 1988, three doctors worked for eight hours to repair the damage to my spine, and I was in a partial body cast for the next six months. Afterward, I had to learn to walk all over again with the aid of a walker.

My doctor would not prescribe physical therapy for me. He said I would just have to learn to deal with the pain. I was taken out of the cast, off of pain medication and given an anticipated recovery period of five years. Then I was released to return to work the next week. Even then, my daily commute was more than a hundred miles a day.

After ten years of chronic pain, I was diagnosed with fibromyalgia. Soon afterward, I was also diagnosed with spondylosis, which trapped three nerves in my neck. This resulted in the complete loss of the use of my right arm and hand. I couldn't hold a cup of coffee or brush my teeth with that hand.

Irritable bowel syndrome then began to play havoc with my digestive tract, and it was also during this time that I was diagnosed with clinical depression, due to an imbalance of hormones in my system. When I got to the point I could no longer bathe myself or walk, I began praying for God to take me home. No oral medication could touch the pain—only painful injections in the pressure points, where the muscles and nerves were so entangled.

1998 was one of the darkest years of my life, but it was at my breakthrough point in which I began to experience the supernatural healing power of Almighty God. Pastor Benny Hinn's TV ministry was a God-send. The Lord used his teachings on healing to bring me up out of a wheelchair and also out of the belly of Hell!

My Mother Acted in Faith

My mother was a prayer partner, and when she had seen me giving up, she called the Benny Hinn Ministries prayer line. She encouraged me to listen to tapes she had received as ministry gifts. On one of the tapes, Pastor Benny talked about anointed music being a key to healing. I was so desperate for some of his anointed music that I prayed for a miracle. I didn't feel like I had enough time to wait for ordered tapes to arrive.

Mother had been so good in taking care of me that I

wanted to buy her something as a special thank-you. I knew she loved the Gaithers, so I wheeled myself over to the music rack at WalMart, while she bought a few items in another part of the store. When I reached down to pick up the cassette tape I decided to buy for her, I couldn't believe my eyes. There was a "Healing" tape from one of Pastor Benny's crusades in Ohio (Cleveland, I believe) right behind the tape I wanted for my mother. I bought the tape and a cassette player and began listening to it as soon as we got home. It was so powerful that I kept playing it over and over.

Within a few days, Mother received a beautiful instrumental tape called "Portrait of Praise" from Pastor Benny's ministry. I decided to buy some blank cassettes so I could record both tapes on one longer cassette. As much as I was playing them, I thought I might need to make backup copies. Over the next several months I wore out three cassette players and three backup copies of the original tapes, while I listened to this anointed music day and night, and it carried me to a new place in the Lord.

I experienced such a powerful healing during that time that I began praying for the Lord to touch Pastor Benny's heart to make a healing tape. I was so excited when I learned that he felt burdened to make a tape series called "Atmosphere for Healing." Although I've had recurring symptoms of fibromyalgia since then try to invade my body, I've continued to fight the good fight of faith.

OTHER MIRACULOUS HEALINGS

I've experienced several other miraculous healings in the past few years. I've had to fight against doctors' reports of lupus, rheumatoid arthritis, chrohn's disease and colon cancer, but *no* weapon formed against me has prospered!

Two weeks before Christmas of 2005, the results of a myleogram and CT scan revealed that I had spurs on my spine that were pinching seven nerves. I was told I needed three surgeries on my spine. One would be to attempt to repair the cervical area (my neck was "gone" from all the ruptured discs), and another for the severe spinal canal stenosis that I was told would eventually paralyze me. Moving vertebrae needed to be stabilized with titanium screws that had not yet been approved by the FDA. I was considered high-risk for possible blood poisoning, high risk for pneumonia (because of my history of bronchitis) and high risk for a stroke (because of my roller-coaster blood pressure). I was also diagnosed with a possible brain tumor.

I remained calm as the doctor gave me these diagnoses, but it was a little disturbing when he told me he was not happy at having to do the surgery with all the risk factors involved. After leaving the doctor's office, I began praying, "Father, that was the doctor's report, but Your Word promises that I was healed at Calvary."

During the week of Thanksgiving, while decorating my Christmas tree, I listened to Juanita Bynum tell of a painful season in her life in which she asked the Lord what was happening to her. He told her that she was in a fiery furnace and for her to "finish the furnace," because she would bring someone else's deliverance out with her. That became my daily prayer, "Lord, help me finish the furnace, and show me whose deliverance is coming out with me."

REACH OUT TO JESUS

A few weeks later, in January, we were having communion in our church. My pastor said that if anyone needed healing, all they had to do was to reach up to Jesus, and He would heal them. As I held the communion cup up to the Lord and asked for my healing, I saw a flash across my spirit of the little boy in the movie "ET," the moment their fingers touched. Electricity and heat began moving up and down my spine, and I felt bones literally moving, as a gentle, invisible hand pressed on my back.

I was praying in the Holy Ghost, and a friend from my discipleship class was interpreting as I prayed, a first for her. As soon as I stopped praying, our pastor spoke the exact words she had just interpreted. People sitting in the row in front of us turned around and looked at us in amazement. We were so far back from the pulpit there was no way the pastor could have heard us!

After the service, I told my pastor what had happened, and he asked me to see if the doctor would let me come back for another visit to confirm that I had been healed. The scheduling nurse refused to make an appointment for me, but I didn't have to have the doctor's word to know I had been healed. I had God's *rhema* word!

THE FIERY FURNACE TRIAL WAS OVER

Since I knew the fiery furnace trial was over, I began asking the Lord whose deliverance was coming out of it. Although I didn't hear anything right away, I kept asking and waiting, knowing that God was not man that He should lie. On February 24th, I received a phone call that literally shook me to the core. It was from the lady who had beaten me and was responsible for all the pain I had suffered in my body. She had heard about my healing and wanted to know if I thought she might be healed, in my church, from the pain that was wracking her own body. Knowing that she had been actively involved in the occult and had sought to have curses put on me for many years, I was terrified of taking her to my church. I didn't know what might manifest.

I began praying in the Holy Ghost and reading Larry Huch's book, *Free at Last: Removing the Past from Your Future* (New Kensington, PA; Whitaker House Publishers: 2000). I felt that Wednesday morning, during our praise and worship service, would be a good time to take this woman to church with me. The Lord then worked a very supernatural miracle, directing me in a prayer of salvation, healing and deliverance for her. It was soaked in tears as she prayed.

As I began entering into praise and worship, I could hear sobs behind me, as the woman prayed for Jesus to show her what He wanted her to do with her life. I saw the most beautiful picture of the value of one soul and thanked the Lord that He would trust me enough to use me in this way.

I bought the woman a Bible and found out later that she was reading it and praying for me every day. What a miracle! It was so awesome, seeing God give me that special forbidden fruit Satan thought belonged to him. That has been a prayer of mine for a long time: "Give me the forbidden fruit that Satan thought was his, let me snatch those helpless souls about to fall into the abyss of eternal Hell out of his hands, and put them into the loving arms of their Savior." This is what I gladly die for in the flesh!

I REFUSE BITTERNESS

I believe the main reason God has blessed me in such supernatural ways is the fact that I work very hard at refusing to allow bitterness to take root in my heart against anyone who has hurt me. Yes, I still get upset with people and even angry whenever I see injustice, but I can't afford to allow bitterness to take root and produce the sin of unforgiveness in me.

God will not allow you to take unforgiveness to Heaven with you. That's the very heartbeat of the cross—forgiveness! I personally believe this may be one reason that some of God's children linger in the valley of the shadow of death. God's mercy may be keeping them until the roots of bitterness are axed so that forgiveness can flow from their hearts—just as it did from the heart of Jesus. *"Father, forgive them"* needs to be our prayer for anyone who has hurt us—even if it has to be our final prayer!

ANOTHER CHAPTER

This story has another chapter. It didn't end on February 26th. On October 31st, I called my mother from work and asked her to pray. The woman was in the hospital, and I had a very uneasy gnawing within me that I couldn't explain. I knew she had been in the occult for many years, and I asked the Lord to please not let anything happen to her on Halloween, since it was synonymous with witchcraft.

The more I prayed, the more intensifying the gnawing became within me. Then I received a phone call at work telling me that the doctor had decided the woman's life was in jeopardy, and so he was having her transferred to a hospital in Atlanta. He even rode in the ambulance with her.

Later one of my co-workers told me that she'd just had something hit her. She called it a premonition. This woman was going to die. When I heard that, my spirit was screaming "noooooo!" I knew I had to get somewhere alone where I could pray outloud. As is my custom, I went to the ladies restroom and asked the Lord to keep everyone out while I labored in prayer. And He did!

I began sensing a very cold, clamminess around me, so I went into a deeper level of prayer. When I finally felt a release, I went back to my office. Later I learned that the lady had suffered a heart attack after arriving at the Atlanta hospital and had been pronounced dead. The doctor decided to try to revive her, and he was able to bring her back to life! Only Heaven will reveal the impact prayer had on that whole process. I'd like to think it was a major key!

A few days later, I visited the lady in the hospital. She told me about having a dream during the time her body was going through such turmoil. She dreamed she was in a morgue and could feel a cold, clammy sensation!

A VISIT TO THE KING CENTER

In October of 2005, along with a very close friend from Belize, Emrese Woodward, I went on a spiritual journey I felt was inspired by the Holy Spirit. We went to the King Center in Atlanta. The memory of Dr. Martin Luther King, Jr. continues to live in the hearts of so many, and you could literally sense his presence everywhere in that place. Before I left home, I'd felt an urgency to take some stones that had been sent to me by my very special friend, Donna Ann Walling. She had collected them on various spiritual journeys and felt that the Holy Spirit had a purpose for them in Atlanta. Some of the stones came from the headwaters of the Mississippi. She had been summoned by the Holy Spirit to pray over these headwaters just eight days before Katrina hit New Orleans.

I felt that the stones needed to be prayed over and released in water, but the only water I'd seen at the King Center (looking at the Internet presentation) was a fountain. Later, I shared my desire with Emrese, and we were both ecstatic when we found a beautiful layered rock waterfall next to a rose garden in the park! We held hands as we prayed and prophesied over each of the eight stones. Then we watched as the water carried each of them away.

They were all different sizes, colors and textures, and I heard the Lord speak very audibly in my spirit that this was the picture of true unity through diversity! We both saw that as a symbol of God raising up eight nations in the city of Atlanta that would walk in unity through diversity. I also sensed a rumbling in my spirit. Denominational walls were crumbling!

There was a second set of eight stones, and I asked the Holy Spirit what to do with them. They were all exactly the same size and color. He directed my attention to a nearby trash can, and I laughed as I called my two daughters to take them away. Giving each one of them four stones, I told them to run as fast as they could, and throw them into the trash. I saw these as religion's description of unity (you must look like this, talk like this, walk like this—separation from others who don't fit into your mold). It was everything Dr. King hated and stood against. Let it be trashed!

Prophetic Words Over Our City

Much has been spoken over our city by prophets. One of the most memorable prophecies came from a very dear friend, Chad Taylor. While visiting the Cyclorama, the Lord told him that Atlanta would burn again, but this time it would be in the Spirit.

I believe it was 1999 when I heard Tommy Tenney say that God revealed that He was going to do something in the city of Atlanta that He had never done anywhere else in the world, and it was because of a widespread hunger for Him in the area. A pastor from Brazil said that he laid his hands on a map of the US and asked God where the next great revival would take place. His hand landed on Georgia, a state he had never visited or even heard of.

I, too, saw a vision of a powerful visitation over our city. It was symbolic of Jesus' prayer for unity in the Body of believers being answered and manifested in the natural, as His words were simultaneously manifested in the Spirit. He said, *"And the glory which thou gavest me I have given them; that they may be one, even as we are one"* (John 17:22). It was the Morning Star and the Glory of God becoming one, producing the Morning Glory, as this glory cloud hovered over Atlanta like a huge spaceship. (The trumpet-shaped morning glory is the most breathtaking when it's responding to the warmth of the sun!)

DAILY COMMUNION

When the Holy Spirit showed me that the burial of flesh we seek was actually being *in Christ,* I began a study on the references in the Bible that refer to us being *in Christ.* The treasures I've found have "boggled" my mind, treasures of wisdom and knowledge, faith and love. All the fullness of the Godhead bodily, we're made complete in Him.

The communion table, where we partake of His life, became very special to me during that season I spent at the cross. I brought my very best bread and wine for the purpose of fellowshipping with Jesus, our Father and the Holy Spirit and to exchange my bread and wine for His. I now look at daily communion as my covenant connector.

That's all I took to the communion table. No prayer requests! Just my very best bread and wine (the crucified body that had just willingly died for Him, and the blood that had just willingly been shed for Him).

I also love corporate communion at church, but there's something about personal daily communion that has changed my life. It seems as if it seals the intimate time I have just experienced with a special holy kiss.

At times it has been difficult to leave because I felt the longing in Christ's heart for more of His Bride to come and fellowship with Him. I could feel the pain in the Father's heart, as well. He yearns for His children to come back to Him—Jew and Gentile—in unity.

My desire was to stay there with Him, but since that wasn't possible, it seemed that the next best thing was to try to encourage others to look at daily communion as a very special time of covenant renewal, a time of going the second mile in our daily walk. It takes a little longer, but, oh, the difference that fellowship makes!

Laden Down with Gifts

The Holy Spirit reminded me that a good king always sends his guests home laden down with gifts of greater value than the ones they bring to him. In this special season of the Bride and the Bridegroom, I sense a great desire from the heart of the Bridegroom for His Bride to come. It's time for her bridal shower, and she has many gifts awaiting her—here on Earth as well as in Heaven. Will you come and unite in fellowship with Him? Please don't wait until it's too late. He said, *"Behold, I come quickly"* (Revelation 3:11 and 22:7, 12 and 20)!

It's time to accept *The Bride's Manifesto.*

CHAPTER 7

THE DEPTH OF THE CROSS

And all things are of God, who hath reconciled us to himself by Jesus Christ, and hath given to us the ministry of reconciliation. 2 Corinthians 5:18

In the spring of 2005, there was a such a hunger deep within my being that I felt I must make one more trip to the cross. I sensed there was a major key I would find to unlock another great mystery concerning the death, burial and resurrection of Christ and the victorious Christian.

A Winter Season

As I began meditating, the Holy Spirit spoke words to me that were a little frightening and yet intriguing. Although it was spring, He told me I was about to enter a winter season of my life, and it would be the most difficult season I'd ever gone through. He said the winds of adversity would be so brutal that things would be broken off of me that I was too weak to turn loose of. Although these winds would try to "uproot" me, a "crosswind" would sustain me—if I went deep enough.

At the very depth of the cross, the Spirit said, I would find revelation of the ministry of reconciliation. He also told me something that was very puzzling—that my "roots" would be blessed and bear fruit.

Our company was experiencing such rapid growth in 2005 that I had to be away from home more than usual. On several occasions, a female co-worker and I worked through the night. The Lord seemed to give both of us supernatural strength and endurance during that season. Although my mother took good care of the girls while I was at work, it was still very difficult for all of us, and her health was not the best.

For a time, my son Ray moved in with us to help out with the girls and do general tasks around the house, but that only seemed to make things worse. To encourage myself in the Lord, as David had, [*"David was greatly distressed ... but David encouraged himself in the LORD his God"* (1 Samuel 30:6)], I began to meditate on the words the Holy Spirit spoke to me concerning my roots being blessed.

I looked up all the references in the Bible concerning roots, and I found one that jumped out at me, so I began meditating on that passage: *"Blessed is the man that trusteth in the LORD, and whose hope the LORD is. For he shall be as a tree planted by the waters, and that spreadeth out her roots by the river, and shall not see when heat cometh, but her leaf shall be green; and shall not be careful in the year of drought, neither shall cease from yielding fruit"* (Jeremiah 17:7-8).

This passage seemed to be a companion to Psalm 1:3: *"And he shall be like a tree planted by the rivers of water, that bringeth forth his fruit in his season; his leaf also shall not wither; and whatsoever he doeth shall prosper."* In Proverbs 12:12, I found: *"The root of the righteous yieldeth fruit."*

THE FAMILY TREE

As I began meditating on those passages, I saw a huge tree in my spirit. It wasn't an ordinary tree; it was a family tree that represented heritage and legacy from past generations.

The trees in these passages had similarities, but one was referred to as male (*"his fruit," "his season," "his leaf"*) and one as female (*"her roots," "her leaf"*). I knew it didn't matter to God if a tree were male or female, because He doesn't see gender. So I dismissed that point.

Both trees were going through particular seasons of their lives, and I knew that was significant. But what impressed me the most in these verses was the way they represented the family tree. It made me wonder. Would the tree willing and able to stand when all others were falling be chosen to preserve the family legacy?

I began to understand, with greater clarity, why our destiny is not just about us personally; it's about future generations and those who've already gone on to be with the Lord. In my walk with Christ, I'm adding to the legacy of the soldiers in my family who fought the good fight of faith before me. Though their course is finished, the race is not yet over. And they're still earning rewards and crowns!

Paul wrote: *"I have fought a good fight, I have finished my course, I have kept the faith: Henceforth there is laid up for me a crown of righteousness, which the Lord, the righteous judge, shall give me at that day: and not to me only, but unto all them also that love his appearing"* (2 Timothy 4:7-8). The writer of the Hebrews declared: *"And these all, having obtained a good report through faith, received not the promise: God having provided some better thing for us, that they without us should not be made perfect [complete]"* (Hebrews 11:39-40).

PAST AND PRESENT DESTINY

Recently, I asked a very close friend, Gloria Nichols, to come to my home so she could pray and prophesy over our family and home. As she prayed, she saw a vision of a picture on a faded white background and the inscription "4-D." I was reminded of something I believe the Holy Spirit had shown me the year before. I think it's obvious that our destiny is dimensional, past, present and future; however, I sensed that there might be a fourth dimension—future perfect.

I know that much of my own destiny was spoken prophetically by my grandmother, and my past and present destiny is also connected to future generations during the Tribulation. Consider this possibility: that destiny will be perfected in the future during the Millennium, when past, present and future destinies return to the Earth to see salvation brought to the Jews. Then, at the end of the age, all destinies will return to their final destination—eternity with our God in Heaven!

GOD'S ANSWER FOR MY FOSTER FATHER

Three days before my foster father went home to be with the Lord, I saw him for the last time. I prayed earnestly that week for God to open a door so that I could pray for him one more time before he died, and I sensed that his time was near. I had been raised in a strict Southern Baptist atmosphere in which women were always expected to be very submissive. They didn't usually pray out loud for men, especially those in authority over them, so I was very nervous about this. When the door opened for me to speak to him privately, however, I quickly ran through it.

I asked him if I could please pray a prayer of blessing over him. He smiled and told me he would love for me to do that. I told him that I had not come for anything but his legacy, but I wouldn't leave without it! When I finished praying for him, I felt like things had finally been reconciled between us after nearly forty-five years. (I will share more of our story in another book I'm writing, *Love Is Death, Burial and Resurrection*.)

Afterward, I learned that he had told my stepmother he wished someone would come by to pray blessings over him. Later that day, his pastor also came to pray for him. God had wanted him to have double blessings that day!

A Very Humble and Godly Man

My foster father was a very humble man disfigured from birth defects. Although he was small in stature, he had become a giant in my eyes. As I prayed for him, I asked God to answer every prayer he had ever prayed for me before I left this earthly body. I don't ever remember a night when I was growing up that Daddy didn't get down on his knees and pray for us—no matter how late he got home from work. He would weep as he prayed and told God how much he needed Him.

My foster mother was severely crippled from rheumatoid arthritis, and yet I never heard either of them complain about anything. They were two of the most godly people I've ever known.

Daddy and his brother owned a small independent grocery store in College Park, Georgia, that flourished while I was growing up. After the airport bought their property, Daddy continued going to the farmer's market to buy produce so he could make sure his older customers had food. He loved people, and his heart was always with those he knew had very little—especially those who lived in Colored Town (as it was then called). And those people loved him—even more than some white folks did. "Mr. Earl" "carried" them food, whether they had money to pay for it or not, until he was forced to quit driving. But by then, he was already in his eighties. He loved people so much that he walked his talk—whether he felt physically up to it or not.

MEMORIES OF CHRISTMAS

Christmas at our home was very wonderful when I was a child. Some of the fondest memories I have were those of helping with the special gift boxes (mostly food) that my foster parents gave so joyfully during the holiday season to those who were handicapped or didn't have much. I remember Daddy's store being filled with dolls and all kinds of toys. He would let his customers put them on layaway for Christmas.

Most all of his customers had credit accounts, and a lot of them owed him quite a bit. Still I don't ever remember hearing him refusing anyone credit to buy food, at least while I was working at the store—no matter how much they already owed.

A STAND AGAINST RACISM

One of the qualities that I most admired about my foster parents was their stand against racism and prejudice. They hated it. Because of my foster mother's health, we had to have a housekeeper come in several days a week. Elberta was my buddy, and I loved her a lot. If Daddy was working during mealtime, I always wanted to eat with Elberta. I loved to hear her tell stories about her family—especially her kids. She always seemed to have so much joy in her heart, and the biggest grin that just made my day whenever I was around her.

DADDY'S UNCONDITIONAL LOVE FOR ALL PEOPLE

Daddy's legacy (that I wanted) was his unconditional love for all people. After he went home to be with the Lord, I asked God to enlarge my tents and extend my boundaries. I wanted this legacy to extend to Atlanta and then to the uttermost parts of the world. I felt that his presence was with me the day Emrese and I went to King Center and prayed for unity. I've had a hatred for racism and the restrictive religious traditions of men for years, and I long to see the day when a spiritual earthquake uproots them all!

MY AMAZING GRANDMOTHER GENEVIA

My foster mother and natural mother were half-sisters. They had the same mother but different fathers. I was named for their mother, Genevia Love. The things I heard about her ministry have made me realize just how important it is for our family legacy to continue, and it's something I pray my children will not take lightly. She was a powerful woman of faith who held ladies' meetings at her home on Wednesdays. My natural mother said she and my foster mother used to play with the children who came with their mothers to hear my grandmother teach and preach the Word of God. Grandmother's meetings usually lasted all day long, and sometimes into the night.

Genevia Love was a woman who loved her Lord, and she went home to be with Him on Valentine's Day when she was just thirty-three years old. She had laid out her burial clothes before she went to bed that night!

SOME HALLOWED GROUND

I sincerely believe that my grandmother and my foster parents hallowed some ground in the College Park-Union City area and planted some spiritual seeds that are bearing fruit today where the powerful World Changers Ministry is based. I often wonder if they are part of the cloud of witnesses occasionally hovering over that area cheering Pastors Creflo and Taffy Dollar on every time a life is changed because of their ministry. We are taught: *"Wherefore seeing we also are compassed about with so great a cloud of witnesses, let us lay aside every weight, and the sin which doth so easily beset us, and let us run with patience the race that is set before us, looking unto Jesus the author and finisher of our faith; who for the joy that was set before him endured the cross, despising the shame, and is set down at the right hand of the throne of God"* (Hebrews 12:1-2).

THE IMPORTANCE OF RELATIONSHIPS

Robert Stearns' book, *Keepers of the Flame:* Unlocking the Mystery of Acceptable Sacrifice (Clarence, NY; Kairos Publishing: 2003), helped me understand the importance of relationships in pursuing your destiny. He said there are four courts, or levels, of relationships, and we should have relationships in all four: the Court of the Gentiles, the Outer Court, the Inner Court and the Holy of Holies. The Holy of Holies concerns the place of covenant where your identity is established and your destiny is released. Ideally, this is where your spouse and immediate family should be, but sometimes that's not where they want to be, or perhaps where they've progressed in their walk with the Lord.

Some people grow much faster in the Lord than others. I sensed that this was what the Holy Spirit was revealing to me about release concerning my family tree and destiny. Covenant relationships are keys to the fulfillment of your destiny, and God will give you those relationships—if your own loved ones won't or can't, at the moment, enter in with you.

THE SPECIAL PEOPLE GOD WANTS TO PLACE IN YOUR LIFE

Pastor Jentzen Franklin has recently published a book entitled *Right People, Right Place, Right Plan: Discerning the Voice of God* (New Kensington, PA; Whitaker House Publishers: 2007). The book also talks about the special people God wants to place in your life so that they can help you reach your destiny. (These are two must-read books for those who are passionate about their destiny.) I have several special covenant friends the Lord has given me who live in different states. One lives in another country. I've had the privilege of meeting three of them face-to-face. These were divine connections whom I know were gifts from the Lord, and we have established personal covenant relationships via e-mail and telephone conversations. They span the globe from Florida to Washington to Minnesota to South Africa. I was not looking for friends at the time any of us connected, but we have all seen the hand of God in those connections. I'm thankful that, as I grow in the Lord, He is increasing the circle of covenant friends who are helping me with the major changes that are taking me in a new direction.

Keepers of the Flame helped me realize that it was not a requirement that a husband and/or any other members of my family enter into the Holy of Holies with me, in order for me to walk in the fullness of my destiny. God will give me the covenant friends I need who will be an encouragement to me, as well as hold me accountable, without any guilt feelings of disloyalty to a husband and family.

I had to accept the fact that, for now, my relationship with some of my family was in the Inner Court. I could love them just as much in that Court as I could in the Holy of Holies, because my love for them all was unconditional.

TRYING TO FORCE PEACE

I stated in another chapter that I believed we were on a spiritual journey back to the Garden of Eden. As I gained more revelation and understanding of reconciliation, I saw another beautiful visual facet of the cross. When we stand with our feet firmly planted in the foundation of Jesus Christ, gazing with spiritual eyes into the face of our heavenly Father, He imparts revelation that we are fully reconciled back to Him because of the finished work of the cross. As we extend our hands to our fellowman on either side, the impartation we receive from the Throne Room flows through us to them and manifests as unconditional love, acceptance and forgiveness. This is what reconciles us back to mankind.

Too many people are trying to make peace happen between themselves and their fellowman, in the hope of creating unity. You can work at creating a peaceful atmosphere at home and work, but there can never be unity without it being Christ-centered. It has to start with Him. You can have a level of peace in your home, if only one of you is walking with the Lord, but there will always be resistance against the one who is trying, because the other one is opening the door to enemy invasion. God's Word clearly states that *a house divided* against itself will not stand (Luke 11:17).

After reading and meditating on covenant relationships being so vital to my destiny, I began envisioning our family tree that was planted by the rivers of water. I thought about the root system and where those roots ran. Many of them were in the river because it takes a lot of water to keep a big tree alive, but a lot of them ran underground to other trees. That's when I started seeing covenant relationships as other great trees the Lord was connecting me to. As our roots connected, we became stronger, because we were helping to support each other's destiny. Although the pathway is different for each one of us, every one of the paths is Christ-centered.

RECONCILED BACK TO ITS ORIGINAL STATE

I also envisioned these great trees as being in the Garden of Eden, the Kingdom on Earth as it is in Heaven. In Heaven, the tree of life has leaves that are for the healing of the nations, and I believe on Earth these trees of life will also have leaves for the healing of the nations. These destiny trees are intended to become dynasties in the Kingdom of God, on Earth as it is in Heaven!

In the Garden, everything has been reconciled back to its original state. God promised: *"I will restore to you the years that the locust hath eaten, the cankerworm, and the caterpillar, and the palmerworm"* (Joel 2:25). The New Living Translation of the Bible calls these pests: *"the stripping locusts, the cutting locusts, the swarming locusts, and the hopping locusts."* According to Eaton's Online Bible Dictionary, there were actually ten different Hebrew words used to describe these very destructive pests. Understanding the destruction such insects caused in the natural made me more keenly aware of the spiritual destruction they have caused to our family trees. Little wonder, then, that we're not producing more fruit of the Spirit and more leaves for the healing of the nations!

RESTORATION AND RECONCILIATION

Two other words intrigued me—*restoration* and *reconciliation*—so, once again I went to my dictionary for help:

- *Restoration*: "renew or bringing back to a former position or condition"
- *Reconciliation*: "to restore to friendship or harmony"

God is restoring *things*, but He is reconciling *people.* There's a big difference in these two words. I guess that's why restoration is never referred to as a ministry. In restoration, God does all the work, but in reconciliation, we have a part. I sincerely believe the final frontier in ministry is reconciliation. That has to occur before we can see worldwide Holy Ghost revival.

THE REVIVAL WE ALL NEED

On Mother's Day, 1985, the Holy Spirit answered a prayer that I had been praying for more than two years. I began reading books and listening to tapes on revival, and after several seasons of prayer and fasting, I laid everything aside and asked the Holy Spirit to show me a picture of revival in the Bible so that I could understand my part in revival.

As I began reading John 11 that morning, I stopped on verse 14: *"Then said Jesus unto them plainly, Lazarus is dead."* I looked back at verse 4, where Jesus had just said, *"This sick-*

ness is not unto death, but for the glory of God, that the Son of God might be glorified thereby." I knew the Bible wasn't contradictory, so I began praying for revelation. Then the Holy Spirit showed me the answer in verse 11: *"Our friend Lazarus sleepeth."* There's a sleep that makes a person appear dead. People who walk in their sleep are in a realm where they're not fully conscious of what they're doing. Likewise, there's a death walk people operate in while they're awake and, again, they're not fully conscious of what they're doing.

But you can't revive something unless it was once alive. Jesus told what happened to Lazarus in verses 9 and 10: he stumbled because his light went out.

Walking in the light is walking in love. Another statement Jesus made seemed to jump out at me. He called Lazarus *"our friend."* That's interesting because He didn't even call His disciples friend until the Last Supper.

After I had meditated several days on this chapter, the Holy Spirit directed me to another chapter—John 20. There I began seeing parallels in the two events. One was a picture of salvation, and one was a picture of revival. I spent several weeks and then several months dissecting those two chapters word by word. It was not until the year 2000 that I heard Pastor Jentzen Franklin describe what the stone represented—offences!

The biggest difference I saw in salvation and revival concerned reconciliation. In salvation, God reconciles us back to Himself, but in revival, He's waiting for us to get reconciled back to Him through Jesus (just as Martha was), then to call our friends back to Jesus so that we can witness the miraculous. When Martha went running to Mary and told her the Master was calling, it doesn't state in the Bible whether or not Jesus had told her to do that. I believe Martha's faith had just been revived, and she knew there was a miracle about to happen that she didn't want her sister to miss!

THE BRIDE'S MANIFESTO

THE SPIRIT-FILLED BELIEVER
JESUS WANTS US ALL TO BE

In John 12, I saw a beautiful composite picture of the Spirit-filled believer that I believe Jesus wants all of us to be. Lazarus was sitting at the table with Jesus, a picture of a disciple. Martha was bringing food to the table, a picture of a servant. Mary was at Jesus' feet, a picture of an intercessor. She anointed Him with costly spikenard, and it released a fragrance that filled the entire house. Then she wiped His feet with her hair (her glory), a picture of an intercessor/worshiper, whom, I believe, had revelation knowledge that those feet were about to shed blood for the remission of the sins of all mankind. Although Mary was sitting at the feet of Jesus on Earth in the natural, it's possible that she was already seated with Him in the heavenly places. She just transcended time.

The tears Mary shed for Lazarus at Jesus' feet, while her brother was still in the tomb, were not in vain. Her pain and compassion so touched the heart of the Master that His body wept in the garden for all those who, like sheep, have gone astray. What a harvest came forth from those tears sown at the Master's feet!

In these last days, it's my heart's cry that we will all look around for the one we can personally touch. I know we all want to see worldwide revival, with millions being saved, but there's always some*one* who is hurting today and God wants to place them in our pathway so that we can love them unconditionally. He is waiting for us today at the depth of the cross where deep calls unto deep!

It's time to accept *The Bride's Manifesto.*

130

CHAPTER 8

WHO IS THE LABORER?

*Then saith he unto his disciples, The harvest truly is plen-
teous, but the labourers are few; pray ye therefore the Lord
of the harvest, that he will send forth labourers into his
harvest.*   Matthew 9:37-38

According to *Strong's Exhaustive Concordance* (#2040), the
meaning of the word Jesus used here for *labourers* is *ergates* or
epyants, "a laborer, a workman or a perpetrator." I found the
following definitions in *Merriam-Webster's Collegiate Dictionary*
for each one of these types:

- *Laborer*: "a person who does unskilled physical work for wages"
- *Skilled*: "learned power of doing something competently. The ability to use one's knowledge effectively and readily in execution or performance"
- *Workman*: "artisan; craftsman"
- *Perpetrator*: "a person who brings about or carries out something"

Have you ever asked the Lord a multiple-choice question, to which He simply answered, "Yes?" Well, that's what I heard when I asked the Lord which type of laborer He was referring to in this passage. He instantly flashed Romans 10:13 across my spiritual eyes: *"For whosoever shall call upon the name of the Lord shall be saved."* I guess this means that whoever qualifies for salvation also qualifies for employment in the government of God.

Peter's Confirmation

Peter seemed to confirm this concept: *"Then Peter opened his mouth, and said, Of a truth I perceive that God is no respecter of persons"* (Acts 10:34). God is *"no respecter of persons."* In other words, you don't even have to fill out an employment application. Your employment is guaranteed. And He offers the ultimate benefit package, and it's all free. No wonder the psalmist declared: *"Bless the LORD, O my soul, and forget not all his benefits: who forgiveth all thine iniquities; who healeth all thy diseases: who redeemeth thy life from destruction; who crowneth thee with lovingkindness and tender mercies; who satisfieth thy mouth with good things; so that thy youth is renewed like the eagle's. The LORD executeth righteousness and judgment for all that are oppressed"* (Psalm 103:2-6).

Although I'm employed by one of the top engineering firms in the nation, their benefit package can't begin to compare with God's. Living in a society today where healthcare costs are soaring to unprecedented heights, just God's healthcare benefits alone (*"who healeth all thy diseases"*) are worth the effort to seek gainful employment in His government.

WHAT DOES IT MEAN TO BE A LABORER?

In my opinion, many people are confused about what it means to be a laborer for the Lord. I used to think that when He spoke of laborers, He was primarily referring to jobs in the church and/or various other ministries. Now I believe there's a greater revelation being released to us concerning God's endtime labors and the laborers needed for them.

Many people are so focused on the church building as the hospital where all the sick and hurting should come for help that they think their duty is ended when they walk out the door of the church. There *are* ministry positions that must be filled in churches, but the harvest is not in the church. It's in the fields, for, as Jesus said, *"the fields ... are white already to harvest"* (John 4:35).

What are these *"fields?"* Perhaps they could be referred to as fields of occupation. If so, the workplace would then present an excellent opportunity for ministry.

ARE WE "OUT OF THE BOX" YET?

We think that we've taken God "out of the box." If so, when we took Him out, we appear to have stayed in it ourselves. Although we talk about taking Him out, our walk doesn't bear witness with our confession. Our boxed mentality tries to keep God where we think He belongs. Since we know that He resides within the temple of the believer, we must become aware that we are symbolic of the Ark, carrying the covenant wherever we go!

I'm praying that greater revelation of this truth will make all of us realize that, from the moment we awaken in the morning until we fall asleep at night, we have everything within us to perform miracles wherever we happen to be!

The world is the vineyard—whether it's standing in line at WalMart, pumping gas at a service station, eating lunch at work or cheering on a favorite sports team. You can sow seeds (words), water them or gather the harvest where someone else has sown and watered—wherever you are! *"Death and life are in the power of the tongue: and they that love it shall eat the fruit thereof"* (Proverbs 18:21).

WORK OUT YOUR OWN SALVATION

The apostle Paul gave us very explicit instructions concerning our salvation: *"The gift of God is eternal life through Jesus Christ our Lord"* (Romans 6:23) and *"Work out your own salvation with fear and trembling"* (Philippians 2:12). According to Proverbs 1:7, *"The fear of the LORD is the beginning of knowledge."* Fear, in this context, is simply a holy reverence for God, so when you work out your salvation in the holy reverence of God, you place great value on His gift of eternal life. You never take it lightly!

Joel Osteen gave another wonderful illustration of working out your salvation, using the fruit of the Spirit as the by-product of our efforts to work out the hardened soil of our hearts.

WORK IS A FASCINATING WORD TO ME

Work is a very fascinating word to me. In the natural

realm, *to work* means "to labor physically," but in the Spirit realm, the seventh day represents the "rest of the Lord" in which we are to cease from our own labors. That seems like an oxymoron, doesn't it? If we are to be laborers, then how do we perform our work if we're resting?

Consider then the words of Hebrews 3:8 and 11-12: *"Harden not your hearts, as in the provocation, in the day of temptation in the wilderness .... So I sware in my wrath, They shall not enter into my rest. Take heed, brethren, lest there be in any of you an evil heart of unbelief."* When the people asked Jesus what they should do, that they might *"work the works of God,"* He replied, *"This is the work of God, that ye believe on him whom he hath sent"* (John 6:29).

ABRAHAM KNEW HOW TO REST IN GOD

I remember the first time I sought the Lord for greater revelation of His righteousness, and He directed me to Abraham: *"And the scripture was fulfilled which saith, Abraham believed God, and it was imputed unto him for righteousness: and he was called The Friend of God"* (James 2:23). How amazing that we can work the very works of God, and walk in His righteousness to a level that we can be called the friend of God, simply by our belief on Christ through revelation knowledge of our position in Him!

Do I have a question mark over your head yet? If not, then you may already know where I'm going with all this. According to Paul's letter to the Romans: *"So then faith cometh by hearing, and hearing by the word of God"* (Romans 10:17). The definition of *faith* is "allegiance to duty or person; something that is believed in with strong conviction." *Belief* is "conviction of the truth of some statement or the reality of some being when based on examination of evidence." Jesus said, *"Now ye are clean through the word which I have spoken unto you"* (John 15:3).

GOOD STEWARDSHIP

One of the most difficult tasks for each one of us who desires to be a laborer for the Lord is good stewardship with our time through self-discipline. We must spend time in the Word and worship of God so that we can learn to discern the voice of God. Just remember this simple formula: $W^2 = V$. Look at the promise God made through Malachi: *"Bring ye all the tithes into the storehouse, that there may be meat in mine house, and prove me now herewith, saith the LORD of hosts, if I will not open you the windows of heaven, and pour you out a blessing, that there shall not be room enough to receive it"* (Malachi 3:10). If He will do that much when we give Him a tenth of our treasure, then how much more will He do if we are willing to give a tenth of our time to Him in our daily walk!

A STEP FURTHER

Let's take this a step further. I want to challenge you to read the fourth chapter of Acts. There the people who were filled with the Holy Ghost sold what they had and brought all the money and laid it before the apostles' feet for distribution, so that there would be no lack in the Body! The tithe, then, is Old Testament or Old Covenant, but revelation of New Testament and New Covenant occurs when you get filled with the Holy Ghost. Suddenly, you want to give everything to the Lord, not just a tenth! When you can get hold of that truth and start walking in it daily, your life will change forever! Abundance will overtake you, and you won't have to wonder when

WHO IS THE LABORER?

or if it's coming. You'll just start looking for people to bless, and asking the Lord to show you opportunities to give.

Jesus rebuked the Pharisees, who gave out of their abundance, but praised the widow, who gave all she had (even though it was only two mites)! And now He's overturning the money tables again. When we give our all to Him, we open up His good treasure. The wealth that's laid up for the just will now be given to the righteous so that we can give out of our abundance! If the Lord of hosts would open the windows of Heaven when we give our tithes, then would He not rend the Heavens and declare them open 24/7 over our lives when we give Him our all?

JUST ONE EXAMPLE

This is just one example of how we can work the works of God. Do you have a deep and intimate relationship with God and know your position in Christ? Do you really believe you will do even greater works than He did? If you don't have that kind of faith yet but would like to take the next step, then ask for it. His Word says we have not because we ask not. Just pray this simple prayer:

Heavenly Father,
I want to have a more intimate relationship with You. Jesus, You said the Holy Spirit would be my Comforter and teach me all things, and He would reveal You. Help me to understand Your Word. Speak to me through Your Spirit, and put Christians in my path who will help me grow to become all that You foreordained and predestined me to be in Christ.

Thank you,
Amen!

GOING DEEPER

If you're struggling with understanding the Bible, get a more modern translation from a Christian bookstore. *The Message* is one that my Mother enjoyed. It's very easy for a baby Christian to understand. Personally I've found the *New Living Translation* and the *New International Version* to be helpful in this regard.

Once you have an easy to understand version in hand, don't start reading in the Old Testament—unless you want to read Psalms or Proverbs. Instead, start with the book of John. It reveals your identity in Christ and His unconditional love for you.

If you are not currently attending a local church, pray for the Lord to show you the church He wants you in for this season of growth. You need to be around other Christians who will help you through your toddler years.

CUMBERED ABOUT

To those of you who may be wondering why you're reading this chapter, you may already have a full plate. My question to you is: "Do you feel like Martha?" Are you *"cumbered about"* with more than your share of duties and responsibilities and wondering why no one seems to want to help you out? Are you screaming, "Lord, where are the laborers?" For me, as they say, I've been there and done that, and I have a dozen boxes of tee shirts to prove it. That's one of the reasons for this book!

If you're like that, then you're laboring over tasks or deeds for the Master's table that you think He will find palatable and enjoyable, but instead of a reward, you get a rebuke. Instead of a kind word, you get a kick in the rear!

Would you like to know why the Lord responds to you in that way? Because you've been sacrificing your time with Him every day to labor over something He didn't ask you to do. Or, perhaps your season is over, and, as a consequence, He's dried up your brook, as He did with Elijah. Now it's time to find the place of your commanded blessing. The psalmist tells us where to find that blessing: *"Behold, how good and how pleasant it is for brethren to dwell together in unity! ...for there the LORD commanded the blessing, even life for evermore"* (Psalm 133:1 and 3).

Perhaps there's a famine in the land, and God has dried up your household finances because He's trying to position you to receive a miracle. Maybe there's no longer unity where you've been residing. Remember, unless the situation appears impossible through natural eyes, it's not an opportunity for a miracle.

IN THE MOST UNLIKELY PLACES

Most of the time your commanded blessing will be found in the most unlikely places and with the most unlikely people. God sent Elijah to a widow whom He said He had commanded to sustain him. This is very intriguing to me because the widow in Zarephath doesn't seem to have received her orders from headquarters. She was getting ready to prepare her last meal, for herself and her son, so they could lie down and die. Instead of them dying, God worked a supernatural miracle so that she could provide for the very man of God who had brought her to her miracle.

Now the woman had more than enough left for her household, and this miracle lasted through the rest of the famine that was even then ravaging the land. Maybe God is showing you that there's a man or woman of God whose brook He's dried up so that He can position you to bless His servant and receive a miracle for your household! That happened to me just recently, and I'm excited just contemplating what the Lord is going to do for all of us!

NOTHING PLEASES HIM MORE

John, in his revelation, wrote: *"Thou art worthy, O Lord, to receive glory and honour and power: for thou hast created all things, and for thy pleasure they are and were created"* (Revelation 4:11). We were created for God's pleasure, and nothing pleases Him more than when we spend time with Him. We must not only know His Word, but we must also know Him, *the* Word.

This word *know*, as used in the Bible, denotes intimacy. *"And Adam knew Eve his wife; and she conceived, and bare Cain"* (Genesis 4:1).

When we really get to know Jesus, we will also conceive and bear fruit, and our fruit will remain. It won't die. In due season, it will also bear fruit, because it already contains the seed of life. In Liberty Savard's book, *Producing the Promise: Keys of the Kingdom* (Gainsville, Florida; Bridge-Logos: 1999) she has a chapter regarding seed entitled *"Apple Tree Destiny"* that will "bless your socks off!" You really need to get all three of her books if you are passionate about your destiny. Although I mentioned this already in Chapter 5, the revelation God has given her about binding and loosing and the way she addresses the soul is worth mentioning again!

MARY AND MARTHA BOTH BIRTHED FRUIT

Both Martha and Mary birthed fruit for the Master's table, however, one was a natural birth (through her own works), and the other was spiritual birth (as a result of the overshadowing and power of the Holy Spirit, because of her worship). I believe that fruit represents souls. Both of these birthing methods are necessary because they give hope to even the baby Christian or the immature toddler Christian that they can also be used by God in this way!

Baby and toddler Christians can always thank God for His many blessings, as they praise Him. As He promised, His *"yoke is easy"* (Matthew 11:30). Martha, quit murmuring and start praising Him [*"the joy of the LORD is your strength"* (Nehemiah 8:10)]. Mary is already worshiping Him, reminding Him who He is to her.

He loves the unity in your teamwork. It's a beautiful sound of harmony in His ears. The angelic hosts are joining you, and together you're dismantling kingdoms of darkness and stripping them of their authority! Blinded eyes are seeing new sights, and deafened ears are hearing new sounds through the signs and wonders that are following this powerful phenomenon!

Think About This

Think about this: many turned to Jesus because of what happened to Lazarus, without any sermon being preached! Pray for Jesus to make a miracle out of your "mess," and watch the light in you throw the breaker on the kingdom of darkness and render it powerless!

I love the revelation the Holy Spirit gave me about another way of looking at the breaker anointing. It's like a breaker switch in an electrical panel, and we have the power within us to throw that switch at any time! It's time to say "lights out" on the kingdom of darkness.

Yes, this sounds like another oxymoron, but it simply means you've disconnected the power source, possibly a soultie, because there's a problem with the wiring. Maybe you've had a faulty connection that's interfering with your anointing. Get it taken care of!

It's time to ask the Chief Inspector (the Holy Spirit) to reveal any hidden agendas the enemy was planning to use in destroying your spiritual house while you were slumbering. Gatherings in homes are already birthing pockets of revival that will start taking entire communities for Christ. We are suddenly reliving the book of Acts!

PRAYER, PRAISE, WORSHIP AND COMMUNION

Prayer, praise, worship and communion brought the Church in during the first century, and I believe the same elements will be used to take the Church out! A restoration of the Tabernacle of David is taking place in homes! This is one reason so many homes and marriages are being attacked. The Pharisee spirit is rising up against the spiritual leaders in the homes, spiritual firefighters are trying to put out the fires, and a mocking spirit is trying to silence prophetic voices.

Whatever opposition the early Church faced, we can be assured that we will face even greater opposition because we are called to do even greater works! But, praise God, if we're to have more opposition, then we will receive greater power, because, *"Greater is he that is in you, than he that is in the world"* (1 John 4:4). You can overcome.

COMPASSION, THE DRIVING FORCE

As we have noted, the Scriptures command us: *"Bear ye one another's burdens, and so fulfil the law of Christ"* (Galatians 6:2). Since God is no respecter of persons, He sees no gender. It's just as important for men to be burden-bearers as it is for women. Men have strong backs and can become beasts of burden, while women carry their life in their bellies. As Jesus promised, out of their bellies shall flow rivers of living water!

Compassion is the driving force that motivates us to keep going back for the spiritual POW's and those who've been left to die in the ditches and trenches. Our oil and wine is within us. It will never run dry, as long as we use it for God's glory and His purposes!

THE CRY FOR LABORERS

Now, back to my original thoughts and the reasons for writing this book. This is a cry for laborers. On March 18, 2003, I had a powerful visitation from the Lord concerning end-time laborers. In the next chapter I will describe those laborers in more detail. It's my earnest desire that you find someone or something you can identify with, and take the next step in your destiny.

Since accepting Jesus as my Savior on February 4, 1983, there have been storms, valleys and fiery furnaces, but the victories have been worth every second of pain I've gone through. Yes, I've gone through all of them. The Valley of Baca (tears) is behind me for now! No more weeping, just worship for this season of my life! *"In every thing give thanks: for this is the will of God in Christ Jesus concerning you"* (1 Thessalonians 5:18). May the Holy Spirit engraft this truth into your heart, and when it happens, your praise and worship will carry you through your Bacas. No one knows for sure what tomorrow holds, but I know who holds my tomorrows. Are you trusting your heavenly Father to hold you and your tomorrow, as you walk down the aisle of your destiny?

It's time to accept *The Bride's Manifesto.*

CHAPTER 9

THE LABORERS

Multitudes, multitudes in the valley of decision: for the day of the LORD is near in the valley of decision.   Joel 3:14

At the beginning of 2003, the Holy Spirit asked me one morning, while I was in deep meditation, how far I was willing to go to set the captives free. I sang my response through a hymn I had known and loved for many years: "Wherever He Leads, I'll Go." When He reminded me that some of the captives were in the belly of Hell, I repeated the song.

Encouraging Myself for the Next Level

I began encouraging myself for this next level by looking back at how the Lord had protected me in 1990 and 1991 when I was taking the Gospel into some of the worst crime areas and drug-infested housing projects in Atlanta. I had gone door-to-door on foot with other ladies in areas where police and mail carriers refused to get out of their vehicles. During that time, I never experienced an ounce of fear for my life or my vehicle. When I spoke to angels to watch over me and my car, I believed what I was speaking.

At the time, I couldn't imagine anything being more fearful in the spirit realm than what I had already experienced in the natural realm. The promise of 1 John 4:18 had delivered me from a stronghold (not just a spirit) of fear, and I didn't believe it was God's will for me to be bound in that tormenting prison again. That promise said: *"There is no fear in love; but perfect love casteth out fear: because fear hath torment. He that feareth is not made perfect in love."* I also believed what Paul wrote to the Galatians: *"Christ hath made us free, and be not entangled again with the yoke of bondage"* (Galatians 5:1).

Over the years, the enemy had used three events in my life and a dream to try and destroy me:

Sexually Molested

At the tender age of five I was sexually molested and threatened with death if I told anyone. No child that age is capable of processing such trauma in a healthy way without a lot of help. The result was that this experience turned my whole life upside down and inside out. The progression of pain and tormenting fear turned into a monster, and by the time I was ten I tried to kill the man who had molested me with a butcher knife!

SEVERELY INJURED

During the same summer I was molested, I fell out of a tree swing with a stalk of sugar cane in my mouth. We were visiting relatives in the country for the summer. I don't remember the extent of my injuries, but apparently the stalk being jammed up into my mouth severely damaged the soft palate of my mouth. What was worse, it took my mother such a long time to find some means of transporting me into town for medical attention that by the time we got to a hospital, my mouth was already infected, and I was delirious with fever.

We arrived at the emergency room, according to the doctors, "just in time." Another thirty minutes, they told Mother, would have been "too late."

Apparently I had also lost a lot of blood by that time because what I remember is leaving my body and floating up to the ceiling. I was looking down at myself lying there in the bed, wondering why I couldn't get past the ceiling. I only vaguely remember the doctors working around me.

Although I don't remember it, I recovered and was able to start school in Georgia a few weeks late. In years to come, I remembered very little about the sexual assault and very little about the trauma of the fall and the resulting infection. My mind had blocked them out. I remembered the train trip to our summer vacation, but I remembered nothing of the return trip.

My mother had taken me home as soon as my fever subsided. My very next memory is from school. I was listening to my first-grade teacher as she held up two dimes to show us how much money our lunch would cost. Mercifully, the rest is a blur, but it left me with deepseated fears.

BEING STALKED

When I was thirty, I was living alone and had my own apartment (because my first husband and I had been divorced) and my sons were staying with a friend during the week while I worked. I was informed by the police that I was being stalked by someone they suspected of being a serial rapist and possibly a serial killer. This brought on a flood of terrible memories from childhood, and I descended into such a vortex of fear that I turned to drugs and alcohol just to get through the long nights.

THE DREAM

A couple of years prior to that, I'd had a dream in which I was reading my own obituary. I remembered seeing a picture of my car in the dream. It had gone out of control on a rain-slicked road and hit a tree.

I already had a fear of water because I'd never learned to swim. (Or was it the other way around?) My high school PE teacher tried to help me learn, but eventually she passed me without learning, saying that I was "unteachable" due to my extreme fear of water.

After my second ovary ruptured in 1978 and had to be re-moved, I went through a severe hormone imbalance. During that season, I thought I was losing my mind. My fear of water intensified so that I couldn't drive to work on rainy days with-out first stopping by the liquor store and buying a bottle of Wild Turkey to help calm my nerves.

I couldn't handle it even when my feet touched a puddle of water. I was so afraid of water that I wouldn't even take a bath in a tub.

One night, as I was taking a shower, the drain stopped up, and water begin filling up in the shower stall. I started seeing scenes from the horror movie *Psycho*, and I too, began to scream..

While all this was happening, the phone started ringing, and someone began banging on the bedroom door. I picked up the phone and started screaming that someone was trying to get into my bedroom to kill me.

Thank God it was my mother on the phone, and it was a family member trying to get into the bedroom. The next day I was taken to a doctor, and he gave me hormone replacement pills. They helped a great deal, but that didn't cure my fear of water.

PARALYZING FEAR

I share the details of this kind of tormenting fear the enemy used against me so that you can see the miraculous liberty I found when the Truth, Jesus Christ, made me free.

I purposely use the term *made me free,* as opposed to *set me free.* A bird is set free from a cage, but it has to decide if it wants to fly away or not. It has this choice. What happened to me was beyond my capacity to understand with my finite mind. The Lord set me free from addictions, by His sovereign grace, but He made me free from paralyzing fear. It had such a stronghold on me that only the Truth, Jesus Christ, could make me free.

I didn't understand just how free I was until I stopped to realize that I had been walking in places where policemen and postal workers feared to walk, and I hadn't experienced even an ounce of fear rising up within me.

During this time, I talked to alcoholics, drug addicts and even a drug dealer in Huntsville, Alabama, who shooed cars away with his hands while he allowed me to minister to him. When I was ministering to these people, I didn't care who they were or where they had come from. My only concern was where they were going!

STILL AFRAID OF WATER

Even though I didn't have any fear of danger while ministering to these troubled people, I still didn't care for large bodies of water. The day I had to drive over one of those mile-high bridges to get to my grandmother's house in Huntsville, I experienced a mild panic attack during the ascent. May son Ray laughed at me because I kept clenching the steering wheel and crying "Jesus" over and over until my wheels were back on level ground.

But the very next day it was payback time. While I was talking to a young man, I caught sight of Ray's nervous leg out of the corner of my eye. It was doing a one-legged Irish jig. After we had walked away from the young man, Ray said, "Mama, didn't you know that was a drug dealer? We might have gotten killed by one of his customers he was shooing away while you were talking to him." It was my turn to laugh, and I told Ray I wasn't the least bit frightened by the prospect.

FREED FROM THE FEAR OF WATER

A few years later I was also freed from the fear of water during a powerful deliverance session with my former pastor, Dr. Mike Johns. The Holy Spirit revealed to him that my fear of water had actually begun in my mother's womb, when I sensed that my father didn't want me. I literally saw myself face down in total darkness, alone in the water.

But praise God, I was gloriously delivered and set free that day, and I witnessed a supernatural miracle when I saw myself turn over, face up to the light that was shining through the darkness of my mother's womb, and I felt the love of my heavenly Father!

My deliverance from this fear was confirmed during my trip to Dog River, when I stepped out on the rocks in the midst of the rushing white water. Only then did it dawn on me that I had finally been set free.

AN INTENSE DELIVERANCE SESSION

Although I knew I was free from tormenting fear, I was intrigued at something that was seen during another intense deliverance session in December, 2007. A friend, Mike Chaille, who was counseling me at the time, told me that he saw fatal automobile accidents as a curse that was placed on my bloodline. After this curse was broken, I began pondering over his comments, wondering if it could mean future accidents, as well as past and present. He even saw in the Spirit a family member who was killed and a passenger who was left paralyzed from an accident.

On December 20, 2007 (just three weeks later), after leaving a Christmas Party with Lauren and Elizabeth, I was having difficulty seeing, as I drove through a heavy rain. After looking down for a moment to turn my defroster on, I looked back up to find a huge tree covering the entire width of the road. I slammed on the breaks, and the car slid into the tree. It was so huge that it stopped the forward motion of the car. The tree had just fallen and had smashed another car before hitting the road. Elizabeth was screaming hysterically.

When I stepped out of my car, I sensed the same eerie feeling I had the night I was awakened while reading my obituary in the dream. It seemed as if I had stepped back in time, and the accident that caused such paralyzing fear to grip my heart then had finally come to pass. The thing I dreaded the most had become reality.

AN ACT OF GOD

When I asked the police officer about the liability (since the tree had fallen from a homeowner's yard), he laughed and said, "Guess you'll have to blame God, since these kinds of accidents are considered 'acts of God.' " I couldn't help but praise the Lord at seeing how He completely diffused the assignment of the enemy that had caused me so much torment. Although my car had extensive damage, none of us was injured.

Later, as I thought about the delay we had experienced at the Christmas party, while everyone was looking for Lauren's present, I saw the Lord's hand in the delay. If the tree had fallen on our car, there's a good possibility that none of us would be alive to tell it. It had "totaled" the other car parked on the side of the road as it was falling. We were spared!

GOING THROUGH THE VALLEY OF THE SHADOW OF DEATH WITH SOMEONE ELSE

In 2002, my foster father suffered a stroke that left him partially paralyzed. To me, it seemed that he was paralyzed with fear. Most of his body functions appeared to be fairly normal for a man in his nineties. I felt so sorry for him that I asked God to allow me to walk through the valley of the shadow of death with him. I had no idea, at that time, that his walk would last the next nine months.

Each day, after praying for Daddy, I would envision us walking through a grassy meadow in the springtime. I was his little girl, holding his hand and telling him constantly how much I loved him, and how thankful I was that he loved me enough to adopt me. I began noticing a peace that seemed to be increasing in him whenever I visited. In an earlier chapter, I shared what happened the last time I saw him alive. God is so good!

UNREST

Around 7:30 or 8:00 PM on December 25, 2006, I began

sensing an unrest, while I was helping Lauren pack for a trip with the church youth group to Gatlinburg, Tennessee. By 9:00 that unrest had grown into a full blown panic attack. I had just pulled into the driveway of a friend, Christine Rosado, who was going on the trip, and I was shaking so hard I had to sit in the car for a few minutes.

Lauren was so upset that she begged me to anoint her with oil and help her say the sinner's prayer again—just in case something happened on their trip. Christine tried to get me to calm down and assured me everything was going to be okay.

I prayed myself to sleep that night (around 10:30), but was awakened at 1:30 AM. I got up and went downstairs to the living room so I could pray. I felt like the Spirit was revealing an assignment against those going on the trip to Gatlinburg, so I prayed in the Holy Ghost. I continued praying in the Spirit as I dressed for work and during my commute that morning.

Not long after I arrived at work, a call came in from one of the intercessors telling me that Jill Jones, a church member who was also a teacher at the Christian school, had died during the night. I asked the Holy Spirit if she was the one I had been praying for. When He said yes, I became very distraught, thinking that I had "messed up" by praying for the wrong person or persons. I grieved over that for the remainder of the week, and the only consolation I could find came when I prayed for Jill's family.

WHAT HAPPENED?

Going to the funeral on Saturday was very difficult, but after talking with an intercessor friend, Gloria Nichols, I found peace. She told me that she had also been in a lot of travail on Christmas night for Jill.

The following morning, before praise and worship service,

I asked the Lord for a special outpouring of His love and supernatural healing for all Jill's family members and friends who were there. I also asked the Holy Spirit if He would please enlighten me as to what happened to Gloria and me on Christmas night and the following morning. For some reason, I felt this was a different facet of what He had already shown me with other experiences, where I had been with loved ones in the valley of the shadow of death. This time I saw something in the Spirit I had never seen before.

This is probably the place where an intercessor faces the most intense warfare possible while still in this earthly body, and it's not to be taken lightly! I believe He was showing me this was the place of final cleansing, through judgment, where the garments are changed. This may be the greatest expression of God's mercy for a child of His about to ascend into the heavenlies. I sincerely believe that before the ascension, that valley must be walked by every child of God. For some this may be accomplished in seconds and, for others, it may take hours or days. Jesus and the angels are with us, and I also believe intercessors are with us in that valley.

I Had Not "Messed Up"

The Holy Spirit showed me that I had not "messed up." Even though I thought I was praying for someone else, He was interceding correctly, because I was praying in the Holy Ghost. Sometimes your mind and spirit may not be "on the same page," but it's always better to pray in the Holy Ghost in a situation like that.

I sensed a court session taking place in that valley. Spirits were being judged and executed, spirits that were sent to steal, kill and destroy from this precious soul. Paul wrote: *"Know ye not that we shall judge angels? how much more things that pertain to this life"* (1 Corinthians 6:3).

CLOTHED IN HER WEDDING GARMENTS

We have been given power over all the powers of darkness, but sometimes I wonder if God uses intercessors to judge spirits for us when we are so bound by grave clothes, even in the valley of the shadow of death. God is no respecter of persons, and I believe that, at her appointed time (see Hebrews 9:27), Jill looked up and saw Jesus standing, as He did for Stephen, with outstretched arms. Then she ascended, clothed in her wedding garment, a robe of righteousness!

MULTITUDES, MULTITUDES

On March 18, 2003, I asked the Holy Spirit to please stir up His gifts within me. While I was reading my Bible, Joel 3:14 seemed to leap off the page. For the first time ever, I heard the Word of God with my left ear, and the voice of God with my right ear. That verse began to echo in my spirit, as if one ear was bearing witness with the other ear.

Because of the use of the word *multitudes* twice in this passage, I knew this verse referred to a lot of people. I began inquiring of the Lord as to who they were and how they would get out of the valley of decision. One word began resounding in my spirit—*resurrection*.

I began contemplating the possibility of God resurrecting a multitude of laborers for these last days and anointing them to resurrect the other multitude before Jesus returns. I started fasting and praying for more revelation from Joel 3:14, and for several weeks, I saw different types of laborers in the Bible. I began meditating and studying these images I had been catching in the Spirit.

There were a total of six types of end-time laborers I saw, but together they form one Church. This is no longer just about a single congregation or ministry or even a great man. It's about the Church of the Lord Jesus Christ.

Each laborer had a powerful corresponding anointing. When I waited for a seventh laborer to be revealed, there was nothing but silence, and when I inquired about the seventh, I sensed the Lord saying that the seventh is the resurrection power of the Holy Spirit, working through them to do the greater works!

A Beautiful Picture of Unity

When I looked through spiritual eyes at the laborers and anointings He had shown me, I began seeing a beautiful picture of unity. It reminded me of a powerful illustration of the *rhema* Word the Lord revealed to me one morning about three years ago. During my quiet time with the Lord, before the rest of the family got up, I basked for several minutes in Zechariah 2:8: *"For he that toucheth you toucheth the apple of his eye."*

When Lauren got up, I told her she was the apple of my eye, and she lit up like a Christmas tree! Things started happening that caused me a delay in leaving for work that morning, and for some reason, I sensed that something special was up.

Shortly after turning onto Highway 92, which would take me to Interstate 20, a fire truck sped past me toward the Interstate. Getting closer to the accident scene, I saw cars turning around because a bridge had just been closed. More emergency vehicles sped past me, as I looked for a place to turn around myself.

The accident had just recently happened, and when I saw the still-blazing car, I heard: *"You are the apple of my eye. No weapon formed against you will prosper."* As I thought about the delay that morning, I wondered if that was an assignment intended for me. I saw the most beautiful picture of my Bible, which had been lying open in a horizontal position in my lap, suddenly close and stand up in a vertical position. The *logos* Word rose up to become the *rhema* Word that had a sudden impact on my life!

It had come full circle. What I received, I sowed. Then it came back to me. But God added so much more to it. I had only sown words of encouragement, but He gave me back the promise of His protection from the enemy's destruction!

OLD VS. NEW

I saw the same illustration between the Old Testament and New Testament with the end-time laborers and anointings. They were literally rising up in the resurrection power of the Holy Spirit, coming together in unity and ushering in the return of our glorious Redeemer! Again, it's like taking the open Bible that's lying in your lap, closing it and standing it up. It's finished. We're just to stand, watch, pray and tarry—in love and thanksgiving. And, in doing so, we shall overcome as we unite.

It's all about unity with Him, through Him and in Him!

Now, let's look at the end-time laborers and anointings the Lord revealed to me. Old Testament laborers have New Testament anointings and *vice-versa*.

THE END-TIME LABORERS

1. Jonah has a John the Baptist anointing, one who is coming out of the wilderness, not with a cry, but with a roar, the voice of the Lion of Judah! The Lamb cries, but the Lion roars! This resurrected, corporate, anointed laborer will take entire cities for the Lord!

2. Lazarus has an Abraham anointing, the friend of God and the friend of Jesus uniting in resurrection power to become an end-time laborer who will help bring about worldwide evangelism and great wealth for the Kingdom of God!

3. The prodigal son has a virtuous woman anointing. Gender is of no significance to God, and women will have kingship authority over principalities. Integrity and uncommon favor will clothe the resurrected prodigals, and they will see a great transfer of wealth for the Kingdom!

4. The dry bones have the corporate anointing of the apostles and prophets. This apostolic/prophetic voice, that literally resounds between Heaven and Earth, is comprised of the Jew and Gentile uniting with such favor that it will see God's glory released between Heaven and Earth! Those who have lost hope and become dry through discouragement and depression will receive a newly resurrected life when they see the blessed hope of glory!

5. Martha, the faithful servant who was the only one looking and waiting for the Lord when He came to perform the miracle upon Lazarus, will unite with an Esther anointing. Martha received great revelation of the resurrection as she walked with the Resurrected One. She will come into the fullness of her destiny, as nations are delivered to the Master's table for the Wedding Banquet because of her faithfulness in serving.

6. A composite Mary—made up of Mary Magdalene, Mary of Bethany and Mary, the mother of Jesus—unites with an Eve anointing to release the ministry of reconciliation. We're on a journey back to the Garden of Eden. Mary, the mother

of Jesus, experienced the physical birth of Jesus, after receiving a visitation from Gabriel announcing His soon arrival. Mary of Bethany experienced revival, after receiving a visitation from her sister announcing Christ's arrival. Mary Magdalene experienced the resurrection, after receiving a visitation from the Master Himself. I strongly believe that these represent the birth, adolescence and sonship phases of our walk/destiny with the Lord. As this laborer unites with Eve, she begins to replenish the Earth with spiritual children who will follow the Master Himself! Each of these women were synonymous with worship, yet each worshiped in a different manner. Mary, Jesus' mother, worshiped Him as she anointed His tiny face with her tears while cradling her little lamb who was destined to become the sacrificial Lamb. Mary Magdalene anointed His feet with oil from her alabaster box, as she worshiped Him, all the while being scorned and ridiculed by the religious crowd. Mary of Bethany anointed His feet with her tears of compassion for her brother who was dead, because she thought the Master had come too late. This is a corporate picture of a warrior/worshiper.

I hope you will take time to pause and ponder over each one of these types of laborers. Can you identify with one or more of them? As I thought about the various anointings that united with the laborers, I realized they were the ones who helped comfort and encourage me while I was struggling in the trenches.

LIKE JONAH, I RAN FROM GOD

Like Jonah, there have been times when I ran from God in prideful disobedience, only to find myself looking up to see bottom! From John the Baptist, I learned that humility and obedience from a heart of gratitude were two of the most powerful keys to the Kingdom. We're still forerunners of Jesus today, for we're preparing the way for His second coming. He didn't come to judge the first time, and neither can we! It's God's will that none perish, but come to a saving knowledge of Jesus Christ. As it was in the days of John the Baptist, there is now only a small window of opportunity to get the Gospel out to the ends of the world, before the Lion of Judah returns. God is no respecter of persons or places. What He did for Nineveh, He can do for Atlanta, Ochlocknee, Minneapolis, St. Paul, International Falls, Nashville, Dallas, San Francisco, Santa Ana, Stockton, Gallup, New York City, Chicago, Kansas City, Houston. Put your city in the list.

A Now Word for This Generation

What follows is a word I received for my son Ray just before his fortieth birthday. I believe it's a now word for this generation:

When I told the belly of Hell to spit you out, I sent you to a dry place. Your dry place is not a place of chastisement, but a place of consecration. I will reveal Myself to you there, and you will hear My voice. I allowed you to feel the subtle bite of the serpent and his other attacks that came suddenly and without warning, striking terror in your heart, for a purpose.

I'm stirring up a tenacious warrior spirit. Just as John the Baptist came out of the wilderness with a cry, eating locusts and wild honey (the very thing that was eating him), and a new revelation of My Word that could not be harnessed by religion, I will bring you out with a roar that will devour the very one who has been roaming about seeking whom he may devour.

John was the forerunner of the Lamb of God, but you will be the forerunner of the Lion of Judah. Your roar, through your extreme worship, will bring terror, as it moves suddenly and swiftly to destroy the evil one's works.

I'm doing a new thing with my remnant of end-time laborers, POW's who've been terrorized and held captive by the enemy. You will not have ministries, but assignments. Like chameleons, you will blend with your surroundings, for I have purposely hidden you for a time such as this.

You must learn to silence your flesh so that when I speak suddenly, you will strike without warning, destroying yokes and bondages that have My people in captivity. You will not be able to plan strategies, nor will you be forewarned of your assignments, for they will come suddenly. For the evil one must also reap what he has sown in this life!

This word came a few days after a very interesting event happened in Ray's life. The week before his fortieth birthday, I had been praying for the Holy Spirit to give me a special birthday scripture I could pray that would bless him and equip him for his destiny. The Holy Spirit gave me Deuteronomy 28. On Ray's birthday, while sitting by a river bank, he heard a powerful wind coming through the trees that sounded like it was breaking them to pieces. Suddenly he heard me shouting in a loud voice, "Devil, turn my son loose! You will not have him! He belongs to God!"

When he called me to let me know what had happened, I told him that it was the exact prayer I had been shouting one afternoon about a year before at home. It makes you wonder if the angels might be collecting our prayers for safekeeping for an appointed time—payback time for the enemy who's tried to delay our answers to prayer like he did with Daniel. God said, *"So shall my word be that goeth forth out of my mouth: it shall not return unto me void, but it shall accomplish that which I please, and it shall prosper in the thing whereto I sent it"* (Isaiah 55:11). We are made in the image of God, and the words we send forth also make a difference!

DEAD, IN A CAVE

I know what it is to be in the cave, just as dead as Lazarus. Criticism and rejection are grave clothes that will suffocate anyone—even the strongest Christian. We must have friends who will speak words of encouragement to us. There's not only encouragement in their words, but power in agreement. You really need Spirit-filled Christian friends to surround you (if your family lives in a negative cave). You respond to your environment. I know this because I'm speaking it from experience.

It's God desire that we prosper and be in health, but prosperity is about more than just money. It's also about the soul: *"Beloved, I wish above all things that thou mayest prosper and be in health, even as thy soul prospereth"* (3 John 1:2).

Abraham had to wait many years for the blessing God had promised him to manifest, yet there was no lack in his life as he waited, because he believed God. Abraham was not perfect. He knew fear and failure, but he never gave up on God, and God never gave up on him. Just like David, Abraham missed the mark when he listened to flesh instead of the Spirit, but neither of them let that keep him down. I believe that when this Lazarus generation comes forth in resurrection power, walking with father Abraham, fear will be dealt a death blow as we see a faith walk from men and women who once were dead, ... "but God."

GET BACK UP AND KEEP MARCHING

Although religion has tried to "disjoint" me and suck the very life out of me by its condemnation and judgment, because of it's laws, the apostles and prophets of the Bible were heroes who have brought me great encouragement and enlightenment. The reason is that I could identify with many of their mistakes. They encouraged me to get back up and keep on marching.

No, their lives were not a bed of roses. Most every one of them was martyred, but there was a comrade spirit among them that enemy forces could not separate. Religion separates the Body, but relationship, through the resurrection power of the Holy Spirit, reconnects the Body together in perfect unity.

God has given me special apostolic/prophetic relationships, and we are connecting with others who have a passionate desire to bring more unity and harmony into the Body of Christ and to help the Bride prepare for her Bridegroom.

LANDING IN THE HOGPEN OF LIFE

The hogpen of life is a very unpleasant place to wake up, yet I'm thankful that when I landed there I did wake up before it was too late. Yes, I believed the lies and was seduced by the father of all liars. I was lured by the material things of this world for a season. I, too, felt like I squandered my inheritance and didn't feel worthy to be treated as a child of the Most High God.

When I came to myself, I just wanted forgiveness. The

open arms of love of my heavenly Father were so precious to me, and He showered me with expressions of His love, a greater understanding and revelation of the virtuous woman.

For weeks I meditated on Proverbs 31, as He revealed insights and a vision concerning this remarkable woman. With the resurrection power of the Holy Spirit, I believe we are about to see those the world considers to be the most unlikely to be used, those who've been faithful with their tithes and offerings, the ragtag ragamuffins who've been sacrificing in order to plant seed offerings for revival and souls for the Kingdom, resurrected as Kingdom financiers!

So Much Work ... So Few Laborers

Many times I've felt like there was so much work to be done and so few laborers to help do it—one of my reasons for this book. During those times I would hear the Lord say, "Martha, Martha." I knew then that I'd been neglecting my time *with* Him to do things *for* Him. Yes, He's concerned with our works for Him, but we can't neglect the most important thing, our daily walk in the Word and prayer that keeps our hearts clean and encouraged.

I noticed two parallels between Martha and the brother of the prodigal son. They were both very busy serving, but their murmuring and complaining caused jealousy to rise up, when it appeared that favor was shown to their brethren.

Esther was a great encouragement in the importance of preparing myself for the King of Kings and desiring His favor. What spoke to me the loudest about Esther was her boldness to prepare the table in the very presence of her archenemy, with a smile on her face because she knew she had found favor with her king. This favor was not because of her outward beauty, but because of her inward beauty, through her persistent preparation. *"Not by might, nor by power, but by my spirit, saith the LORD of hosts"* (Zechariah 4:6). It's time to set the table!

WITHOUT A HUSBAND

All three of the Mary's I saw who were so impacted by Jesus didn't appear to have a husband. I know there's been a lot of speculation that Joseph had already died before Jesus was crucified, so that would have left three women who had no man to go before them into the Temple. I've been in many churches and around a lot of Christian hypocrites, who made me feel like I was an outsider because I was not with a husband. These include Pentecostal churches.

These three women, as a whole, were with Jesus from birth to death, and they served Him with total abandonment. I don't find any evidence that they ever turned away from Jesus. To the contrary, they loved Him with all their hearts.

One of the most powerful articles I ever read that expresses total abandonment and commitment to the Lord was written by Madame Jeanne Guyon. As this book goes to press, "The Way to God and of the State of the Union" is available for reading on www.passtheword.org. If it is no longer available there, search for it elsewhere. It's worth reading.

A REMNANT OF WOMEN

I believe there is a remnant of women in this world who are so totally abandoned to Jesus that they love Him more than they love life itself. Although they are widows—whether literal or just "grass widows," due to divorce or abandonment—I sense that they are uniting with a fresh new Eve anointing that will be so powerful it will resurrect the ministry of reconciliation.

Men who have abandoned the Lord, for whatever reasons,

will come running back to Him as quickly as Mary did to Jesus when Martha told her that the Master was calling for her. May there be a clarion call from this corporate laborer that awakens the Adam of this present generation to the reality of responsible, right relationship to his God, his family, his brethren and his world!

THINK ABOUT IT

Think about what's happening with the current war in Iraq, and look at the spiritual parallels. War will wear you out. I don't care how much training you've had or how much artillery you have, the enemy's persistence will eventually take its toll on you. You need a time of R and R. But this R and R is not the human rest and relaxation; it's Jesus' rest and His resurrection power!

Reinforcements are needed to relieve those who've been on the frontlines. Special services are needed to rescue the POW's. Letters of encouragement from loved ones are vital for morale. And communication lines must not be disrupted.

It's time for the end-time laborers to wake up, get up, stand up and run to the vineyards. Multitudes are standing on the edge of eternity. It's much later than we think. The midnight hour is fast approaching, so don't tarry. RRRRRRRUUUUNNNN!

It's time to accept *The Bride's Manifesto.*

CHAPTER 10

THE MANDATE

For the gifts and calling of God are without repentance.

Romans 11:29

If we are called by Christ to do the greater works, and we are (see John 14:12), then we have the same mandate (an authoritative command) as Christ had! God has given us many gifts, but one calling—the same one as Christ had. That these gifts are *"without repentance"* simply means that He will not change His mind about the gifts or the calling.

Even Jesus Had to Grow

Jesus didn't come into this world fully grown, as Adam did. Instead, He was born of a woman. He was a baby who cried and had to be fed, just like each one of us. The Word became flesh so that He could teach us, by example, how to be the flesh destined to become the Word. Paul wrote: *"And be not conformed to this world: but be ye transformed by the renewing of your mind, that ye may prove what is that good, and acceptable, and perfect, will of God"* (Romans 12:2). It is God's will for us to be transformed (changed) by renewing (restoring) our minds. Sin has so fragmented our minds that we've lost our true identity. Our minds are like Swiss cheese.

The Lies of the Enemy

We're hiding behind so many facades, trying desperately to discover who we really are, and yet we've believed the lies of the enemy: "It's my life, so I can live it the way I want to live it." "Live fast, love hard, die young." "Take what you want, even if it belongs to someone else." "Do unto others before they do it to you." "Nobody will ever know what I do in secret." "I'm not hurting anybody else." "I don't need God. After all, He doesn't answer prayer because He didn't heal my Daddy when I asked Him to." "If God loved me, why didn't He stop that man from raping me when I was little?" "Why did God allow 9/11 to happen to America?" Your list may vary some, but the idea is the same.

Very little is recorded in the Bible about Jesus from the time He stood in the Temple, reading from the scrolls at age twelve, until He began calling His disciples and His baptism by John the Baptist. One of His earliest acts, upon assuming His earthly mantle, was to declare His mandate. He did this in the synagogue in Nazareth. I am convinced that the words He read that day from Isaiah are our mandate as well: *"The Spirit of the Lord GOD is upon me; because the LORD hath anointed me to preach good tidings unto the meek; he hath sent me to bind up the brokenhearted, to proclaim liberty to the captives, and the opening of the prison to them that are bound; to proclaim the acceptable year of the LORD, and the day of vengeance of our God; to comfort all that mourn; to appoint unto them that mourn in Zion, to give unto them beauty for ashes, the oil of joy for mourning, the garment of praise for the spirit of heaviness; that they might be called trees of righteousness, the planting of the LORD, that he might be glorified"* (Isaiah 61:1-3).

THREE CYCLES

There are three cycles, or phases, also referred to as three days, in the life of a Christian. My desire is that every person reading this book will identify what day, or cycle, they're in now and move on to the next one.

When a person becomes born again, they become a baby Christian. Just as a natural baby needs daily care and nurturing, so does a baby Christian. God wants you connected to mature Christians who can feed you and pray for you until you learn how to feed yourself daily on the Word of God. If you're not in a good Bible-believing, Spirit-filled church, then you need to pray and ask God to show you one. It's His desire to do that.

THE TODDLER STAGE

The next cycle is the toddler stage—corresponding to what the world terms "the terrible twos and threes." This is the day of the desert in your life when your will is being broken, and you're learning how to depend upon God. You're trying to walk, but you keep stumbling when you try to go too fast. God's promises are new and exciting, but you can't afford to run ahead of Him, or you'll fall.

A desert is a dry place, so you need water. Jesus is the Water of Life, and you must learn how to drink from Him often and slowly. Bread and water is your mainstay; meat will not digest well in the desert.

THE THIRD STAGE

When you finally get to your third day, your Promised Land is in full view, but there's a raging river to cross, and its banks are overflowing. This is where you learn to step out in faith and watch God supernaturally make a way for you to enter your Promised Land. You may have to camp out by the river for a season while you learn how to engraft God's Word.

Faith requires you to take the first step into an impossible situation. If you can see the solution with your natural mind, it's sight, not faith. The first verse I asked the Holy Spirit to engraft into my heart was this: *"In every thing give thanks: for this is the will of God in Christ Jesus concerning you"* (1 Thessalonians 5:18). That was in 1983, and this word is still being tried and tested in my life today.

You must learn to trust God, and see His hand in everything that happens to you—good or bad—because the enemy cannot touch you unless he has permission from your heavenly Father. You've been hedged by Him, and He promised not to put more on you than you could bear and to never leave nor forsake you. The Word is there, spoken by God Himself, but the problem is with us. Do we believe it?

YOUR PROMISED LAND

The Promised Land is not the Garden of Eden. No, it's not a rose garden. Quite the contrary! I'm not trying to give a bad report, but you need to hear both sides of the report. Yours is a land full of giants, mountains and valleys, stormy seas and fiery furnaces; but it's also a land flowing with milk and honey and the biggest and best fruit this side of Heaven!

It's the land of golden opportunity, where a little unknown shepherd boy can become a world-renowned giant slayer and a great king, or a little orphan girl can become a queen and see nations delivered from death. It's a land where outcast prodigals find love, acceptance and forgiveness, a land where dead marriages, relationships and families find new life through reconciliation. It's a safe haven for harlots who've found redemption. They're blessed and highly favored by the King of Kings, as they worship at His feet. Go on, take your Promised Land!

MINISTRY IN EACH CYCLE

There's a mandate for ministry in each of the three cycles. Baby Christians are full of joy and excitement and bring many to Christ because of their testimony. Their childlike faith gives an opportunity for Jesus to perform many miracles in their lives. They rest a lot and are happy with just the presence, not presents, of loved ones being around them.

When we take the time to invest in the lives of baby Christians, it actually benefits us, because they will usually do unto others as it has been done unto them. Thus you will have spiritual grandchildren who will bring you earthly blessings and heavenly rewards.

The toddler Christian is the most difficult to be around,

and that's where the majority are, wandering around in the wilderness, constantly murmuring and complaining about everything they don't have. These will wear down even the strongest Christian. Look at Moses, for example. God even got fed up with the murmuring and complaining of those Moses led, and He would have wiped all of them out if Moses had not pleaded for mercy for them.

Many such wanderers are the product of blended homes or dysfunctional families where there was a battle for a balance of love and harmony—if it even existed. They're insecure, and simply don't know how to work together during tough times.

Love is a word that is not easily defined to insecure people. Most of them put a price tag and/or conditions on it. They don't understand God's unconditional love, and His command: *"Love your enemies, ... and pray for them which despitefully use you"* (Luke 6:27-28).

LOVING THE UNLOVELY

It's very difficult to encourage chronic complainers, but we have a mandate to love the unlovely and spiritually autistic, who don't know how to receive love. And we're to love them unconditionally, without expecting anything in return. When you live with a spouse and/or children who are in the wilderness and don't want to grow, because they're so full of stubbornness and rebellion, then you need to pray for God to give you healthy friendships that will be an encouragement to you. Otherwise your own family will eventually cause you to become discouraged.

In spite of the difficulty for the child of God in this phase, many supernatural miracles are seen in their lives. It's my personal belief that His greatest demonstration of grace and mercy is extended to us during that particular period of growth.

A LIFE OF ADVENTURE AWAITS

There's adventure in the Promised Land if you're willing to partner with the Holy Ghost and the heavenly hosts. The Angel Express will take you places your own finite mind has difficulty processing, but the mind of Christ sees it clearly!

Boring and *mundane* will no longer be in your vocabulary. Instead, you will find keys to unlock mysteries. As you sit for longer periods in the heavenly places with Christ, you will begin to see things from God's perspective, and the giants around you will become as mere grasshoppers—even as small as ants.

GLORYING IN TRIALS AND TRIBULATIONS

The Holy Spirit revealed something to me on July 5, 2007 that was an eye-opener. He reminded me that the apostle Paul said he gloried in trials and tribulations. Instantly, I saw the *"thorn in the flesh"* (2 Corinthians 12:7) he spoke of as the price for revelation. When Saul of Tarsus quit *"kick[ing] against the pricks"* (Acts 9:5) he started kickboxing Satan. This enemy is already under our feet, but we can still kick him out of the way when we need to. After Paul prayed three times for God to remove the thorn, or pricks, from his flesh, God told him it was there to buffet him against pride, because of the revelation he was receiving.

The Holy Spirit told me I could have a comfort zone or I could have revelation. It was my choice. More thorn pricks release more revelation. As I thought about the crown of thorns placed on Jesus' head, I realized that's why we desperately need His mind. I still spend time in the Word, but I desire more time with *the* Word, sitting in the heavenly places with Him.

I love the global panoramic view of what's happening on Earth. No, this is not about New Age, out-of-body travel. Jesus said the Kingdom of God is within us. We must place Jesus on the throne of our hearts daily and proclaim that He is King of Kings and Lord of Lords in our lives.

LOOKING WITHIN

When we draw nigh unto God, we don't look up; we look within our own hearts: *'Be silent, O all flesh, before the LORD: for he is raised up out of his holy habitation"* (Zechariah 2:13). God raised Jesus up from the dead after three days, and we are now in the third millennium, the third day. So this is resurrection day for us!

God promised to fill all the earth with His glory: *"But as truly as I live, all the earth shall be filled with the glory of the LORD"* (Numbers 14:21). And how will He do that? He said: *"Be still, and know that I am God: I will be exalted among the heathen, I will be exalted in the earth"* (Psalm 46:10).

What would happen if we all started reserving more still time, apart from our daily walk, quality time away from interruptions, at a time and in a place where we could silence our flesh and ask God to arise? As we noted in earlier chapters, we have the power within our own tongue to speak life. James wrote: *"Ye have not, because ye ask not"* (James 4:2). Is it possible that God is longing for us to remove the stone and open the door of our own hearts and ask Him to come forth and manifest His glorious presence? Could He be waiting for us to speak resurrection life to Him, who dwells within us? Has our own flesh buried Him with words of unbelief? Think about it!

ARE YOU CONTENT WITH LIFE AS IT IS?

Are you content with your life as it is, or do you want God to perform great exploits through you? I've been on a quest now for the past twenty-five years, discovering God, and yet I feel like the journey has just begun. I sincerely pray that, in these few pages, you've been able to see some of the WOW in God that I've discovered. I hope the book has stirred embers within you that are beginning to rekindle and burn with passion even now for Him.

Always remember, He's no respecter of persons. What He did through the great heroes in the Bible, He will do for us, all of us who are willing.

WAITING ON GOD?

A very popular passage from Isaiah says: *"But they that wait upon the LORD shall renew their strength; they shall mount up with wings as eagles; they shall run, and not be weary; and they shall walk, and not faint"* (Isaiah 40:31). As popular as it is, however, this passage has been misunderstood by many. We're not *"wait[ing] upon the LORD"* when we kick back in our recliner and use the que-sera-sera (whatever will be will be) mentality as our excuse for not laboring. That is not "waiting"; it's slothfulness. And God will not bless a lazy person!

"Wait[ing] upon the LORD," in this context, means serving him, just as a waiter or waitress in a restaurant serves. We do whatever needs to be done for the Body of Christ, knowing that whatever we do for the Body, we are doing for Christ Himself. *"And the King shall answer and say unto them, Verily I say unto you, Inasmuch as ye have done it unto one of the least of these my brethren, ye have done it unto me"* (Matthew 25:40).

Jesus said: *"Watch ye therefore, and pray always, that ye*

may be accounted worthy to escape all these things that shall come to pass, and to stand before the Son of man" (Luke 21:36). *"And he cometh unto the disciples, and findeth them asleep, and saith unto Peter, What, could ye not watch with me one hour"* (Matthew 26:40).

One of my favorite songs is "Prayer is the Key to Heaven, but Faith Unlocks the Door." If you want to unlock Heaven, your faith must have a prayer key that you carry with you everywhere you go. You must develop a prayer life, not just a time for prayer, but a lifestyle of prayer in which you are always looking and listening for a need your prayer of faith can meet.

LEARNING TO WATCH

At the end of October, 2006, a very close friend of mine, Kathy Howse, gave me a set of Billye Brimm's CDs to listen to regarding prayer. I had seen Billye appear on television with Gloria Copeland several times, so I was already familiar with her passion for prayer. I listened to the CDs several times, but I was especially drawn to her teachings on "The Watch." On November 6th I began asking the Holy Spirit to give me revelation of "The Watch."

As a member of our Intercessory Group at church, I already knew that we were watchmen on the wall, but this seemed like a different position. I began feeling a heaviness when I prayed in the Holy Ghost, and each day it grew heavier. By Wednesday night at church, I asked Kathy to pray for me. I knew I was grieving with someone, and I sensed the death angel nearby. Still, the burden kept getting heavier and heavier. I even woke myself up during the night several times that week, praying.

I was like a zombie at work on Thursday. Finally, I prayed

desperately for the Holy Ghost to show me who I was praying for so that I might be able to send them a word of encouragement, and He did. On Friday morning, I received an e-mail from Chad Taylor of Consuming Fire Ministries. As I read Chad's e-mail, urging partners to pray for his very close friend, Dr. Winston Moss in Port Elizabeth, South Africa, I knew this was the one I'd been praying for.

I found out later that Dr. Moss had been going through a very difficult season in his life. In the words of Chad Taylor, "Dr. Moss is a prolific Bible researcher, whose biblical studies, research documents and commentaries have been commissioned by leading ministries in South Africa and America. For the past thirty years, Dr. Moss has been teaching the Word of God as a national and international speaker in churches, Bible colleges and seminaries."

After reading so much about this great man of God, I realized that none of us is immune to discouragement and depression. Thus, the need for friends. Our amazing God showed me that if there's not a friend close by, He will divinely connect us with one—even if He has to cross the waters in order to do it!

The result is that Dr. Moss has become a very close friend and mentor, and his encouragement has been a key factor in me having the courage to write this book. What makes this story so amazing is the fact that Chad and I had lost contact for over a year after his computer crashed. He was in New Orleans for quite a while, helping with ministries there after Katrina hit, while I was working long hours and trying to take care of my family.

A few days before I got Chad's prayer request for Dr. Moss, I received another e-mail from him. He told me that the Holy Spirit had him jumping through hoops trying to find my e-mail address, so that we could reconnect. If Chad had not been persistent in searching for my e-mail address, it makes me nervous to think about what might have happened.

Chad is the one who saw a vision, on October 13, 2004, of me writing this book. I still have the e-mail he sent me. It's one I'll always cherish because I know the Lord gave him the vision.

THE LEGACY OF DAVID BRAINERD

Donna Ann Walling is one of the closest friends I've ever had. Although we've been friends now for more than three years, we never met face-to-face until our trip to California in September of 2007. When the Lord connects you, it's a heart connection that has nothing to do with the flesh.

I've never personally known another woman with the heart for revival and healing for the Native Americans as Donna has. Her passion reminds me of the great David Brainerd. "David Brainerd taught a lesson that should be learned by all Christians. Your life doesn't have to be long in order for you to leave a mark on history. David did not let his hard times, the deaths, the sickness, the expulsion bring him down. Instead, he trusted in God and did His will. In his last four years, he was able to impact so many people. Today, his legacy still lives on to show the world the hope that comes through following God's will. The life of David Brainerd is without a doubt a life well lived." On March 25, 1742, David Brainerd left his church to devote his life to the Indians. On October 9, 1746, just four and a half years later, he spoke his last words: "He will come, and will not tarry. I shall soon be in glory; soon be with God and His angels." (From an article by Nit Nosotro found at www.hypterhistory.net)

What a testimony! And all in four and a half years! Do you have a burning desire to impact this world for the Kingdom of

Christ? Is there a driving force within you that keeps whispering, "Something's missing?" Do you look around at your possessions through different eyes than you did even a year ago? Do they now seem unimportant since learning of the sudden death in the family of a dear friend? Small children are suddenly left without a mother. A grieving father is still searching for answers. Parents and other family members are still wondering, "Why, God?" Would your life be different if you found out you only had a year to live?

SOME FOOD FOR THOUGHT

I sincerely pray that this book, especially this chapter, has given you some food for thought. You can make a difference if you desire to do so. Madalyn Murray O'Hair was one woman. If she could make the impact she did, because of her hatred for God, imagine the impact you could make because of your love for Him! *"But as it is written, Eye hath not seen, nor ear heard, neither have entered into the heart of man, the things which God hath prepared for them that love him"* (1 Corinthians 2:9).

When Jesus was on the cross, He showed us the power in connections in His last moments. When He told John, *"Behold thy mother"* (John 19:27), Jesus was releasing those He loved the most so that He could complete His own destiny. He also made a divine connection for John, which would later help him step into the fullness of his own destiny (when he wrote the Revelation of Jesus Christ on the Isle of Patmos).

No one knew Jesus better than His own mother. I'm sure Mary spent many hours sharing the silent years in the life of Jesus with John, things that were not revealed in the Bible. I sense that she now embraced John as the beloved, just as Jesus had. I personally believe these two humble people were probably closer to the heart of Jesus than anyone else He knew in this life. They were the last two people He spoke to before His final words to all mankind: *"It is finished"* (John 19:30).

Passionate About Connections

I can't think of another servant today who is more passionate about network relationship connections in the Body of Christ than L.D. Oxford. L.D. is the founder and director of Joshua AP Network Ministry and E-list and has labored through some of the worst life-storms of any person I know—all without ever giving up. He also realizes that people want to know what God is saying to His apostles and prophets today, so he continues to build the Joshua Apostolic Prophetic Network Ministry, which includes the fast-growing Joshua AP Network E-list, spanning the globe with apostolic and prophetic messages which are sent out over one hundred and fifty global news feeds.

The Lord is blessing L.D. with unique ideas to bless his readers, writers and networking ministries. My prayer is that one day soon he will have all the much-needed support—financial and staff—that he needs, and will no longer have to operate on such a tight budget and have to do most of the work himself.

Burdened for Many Ministries

My heart is burdened for many ministries. Men and women of God are giving their very lives for the Gospel's sake, and it grieves me that they have to literally beg others to help support their work. I realize that you have to use wisdom and discernment, but God is not short on either one. Sometimes I feel that we just have an abundance of excuses for not helping others more.

How many of us would be willing to leave our homes to go wherever He leads? My heart aches for people like Heidi and Rowland Baker, Reinhard Bonnke, Benny Hinn, Rod Parsley, James and Betty Robison and others who are risking their very lives to go into third-world countries to carry the Gospel of Jesus Christ. They minister to precious souls who are starving to death—physically and spiritually. They literally come against the very hoards of Hell in countries where false gods and idols have held people captive for generations. I can't begin to fathom the warfare their ministries continuously face. Yet they keep persevering!

PRAISES FOR TBN

In my opinion, Jan and Paul Crouch have been two of the biggest blessings to the Body of Christ here in America and around the world. They've remained steadfast in their efforts to get the Gospel on TV in the furthest reaches of the earth. I've personally had a smorgasbord to feast on from the hundreds, possibly thousands, of great teachings I've watched on TBN.

I'm so grateful that shut-ins, like my own mother, have been able to go to church through television, when they weren't able to physically attend church. While Mother lived with me, TBN was always playing on her TV upstairs or mine downstairs while I was at work.

Just knowing how God used TBN to capture Chad Taylor's heart during an interview Jan and Paul were having with T.L. Osborn would be enough to shatter any doubt concerning the anointing on their lives. I hope you will read Chad's powerful testimony on his website, www.consumingfire.com, where he shares how God used Jan, right in the middle of their intense interview and just as he was about to flip the TV channel, to speak to him. Not only did He use Jan, but He also used T.L. Osborn to tell Chad that, although the devil had him around the neck, he had an anointing on his life to preach the Gospel. Anyone who knows the now Chad knows that mandate did not fall on deaf ears!

JAN'S CHICKEN STORY

I love Jan's chicken story. Several years ago, my grandsons, Jake and Cory, had a puppy that suffered a severe injury which required immediate surgery. Their father, my youngest son Jason, told the boys there was no way they could afford the money for the surgery. The puppy would have to be put to sleep.

When Jake and Cory told me what their dad had said, I told them Jan's chicken story. They were filled with excitement, and their faith began to soar, and the three of us prayed in agreement, believing that God would do the same thing for their little puppy as He had done for Jan's little chicken.

Later that afternoon, I got a phone call asking me to come over to their home and see the miracle. The vet had called Jason shortly after we prayed and told him that something had happened to the puppy, and he could come and take him home. When I walked over to Jason's home (they lived next door at the time), I saw the puppy in their front yard. He was running and doing flips, while my grandsons playfully chased him around!

TRANSFERRED ANOINTINGS

I realize there are multitudes of unsung heroes who may not have household names, but they are not going unnoticed in the chronicles of Heaven. There have been three occasions when I was in a position to receive a transfer of powerful anointing from mighty servants of God that impacted my life then and continues today, as God stirs and releases the anointing whenever it's needed.

As I noted in an earlier chapter, from Pastor Rod Parsley, I received a mighty deposit of the breaker anointing. From Silvania Machado's holy kiss, I received a deposit of the spirit of humility. And from Pastor Bob Shattles, I received a powerful deposit of the baptism of fire.

Pastor Bob, who was a very close friend of Ruth Heflin, had a glory dust anointing that increased to a glory dust rain shortly before his death. During his revivals, creative healing miracles were beginning to manifest.

Pastor Jim Shattles, Bob's son, was told by a powerful prophet that the Lord was releasing an anointing over his life, in which he would see double the miracles his father had witnessed. Jim's wife Angie has a powerful anointing in releasing the fire of God and financial blessings into the lives of believers. When Angie told me that Suzanne Hinn's father told them Souls Harvest (their church which I attended for a time) was the best kept secret in Douglasville, we started praying for the Lord to reveal what was hidden and to noise it abroad. I believe the Lord is doing just that. Their amazing growth is a testimony to God's faithfulness in what He promises.

We're taught to be careful who we allow to lay hands on us and pray for us. Because of that, I greet many people either with a holy hug or a handshake (as is appropriate), but I'm very cautious as to who I allow to lay hands on me. Whatever prophecies are spoken over me are immediately released to God for His perfect timing in their becoming reality. Occasionally, I will revisit a prophecy (if I feel it's time for it to begin manifesting in my life). I did this last year with the prophecy Chad Taylor spoke concerning the writing of this book.

An Even Greater Impact

As powerful as these transfers of anointing were, I experienced something recently that made an even greater impact on my life. Pastor Ricky Perkins, under the direction of the Holy Spirit, removed his suit coat and had someone place it on my shoulders. He told me the Lord said that when his mantle touched my back, I would receive a transfer of the anointing that was on our church, Deliverance Center of Georgia.

As soon as the coat made contact with my back, I got a glimpse of Pastor Ricky's hand trying to make contact with my forehead, but I was down before he could even touch me. Fire and ice enveloped my entire body at the same time, and I got so drunk I could barely stand up. I had great difficulty walking straight after I finally did get up. I kept going in circles backward! I'm praying that this same anointing will be released through this book to help you bring deliverance to others.

Something Interesting about Revelation

I learned something very interesting from my friend Winston Moss about revelation. The Holy Spirit spoke to him several years ago about dangers in soulties that are formed when revelation is shared with others. At that time, he was teaching in a seminary, and he said that some of the students got very emotional at some of the things that were being revealed. The Holy Spirit told him that it was necessary to break soulties immediately; otherwise, the students would get locked into that particular revelation and not be able to receive greater revelation later.

He and I believe this is one reason the Holy Spirit is revealing so much to us in our chats. Soulties are immediately broken so that we don't get locked into whatever has been revealed. We both want more!

I HOPE IT HAS MINISTERED TO YOU

I hope this chapter has not been difficult for you to understand. It has ministered to me in a new way even as I've written it. Jesus said, *"I must work the works of him that sent me, while it is day: the night cometh, when no man can work"* (John 9:4). And Paul added: *"Walk in wisdom toward them that are without, redeeming the time"* (Colossians 4:5). We are on God's timetable, and many believe we are in the eleventh hour. The Bridegroom comes at the midnight hour. Get ready!

Donna and I have been seeing 11:11 quite frequently, mostly on clocks. Some of the interpretations of this prophetic hour include: "worldwide judgment, latter-day world evangelism, and God's last-day army being launched to go forth in power—her finest hour!" The one that intrigued me the most was "a wake-up code or beacon; it tells you that you are about to make a significant shift or change in your life, and that the change or shift is critical to your destiny." (From an article by Bill White found at www.synchronicityexpert.com)

Do you fear God? Do you believe He's not only a God of mercy, but also a God of judgment? Jesus left a warning that every person would be wise to heed: *"But I will forewarn you whom ye shall fear: Fear him, which after he hath killed hath power to cast into hell; yea, I say unto you, Fear him"* (Luke 12:5).

LABORERS BEING SOUGHT

Many laborers are being sought by the Lord and summoned to this final hour: *"And about the eleventh hour he went out, and found others standing idle, and saith unto them, Why stand ye here all the day idle? They say unto him, Because no man hath hired us. He saith unto them, Go ye also into the vineyard; and whatsoever is right, that shall ye receive"* (Matthew 20:6-7). There are many who've been rejected by religion and are wandering around without vision or hope. I earnestly pray that you will ask God to put someone in your heart who's wandering. You could be praying for another Jonah or Peter whom God is ready to use to impact the world for His glory!

On the morning of July 10, 2007, at exactly 3:00 AM, the Holy Spirit woke me up. I was seeing 11:11 in my dream realm, but it was without the colon. I started writing down words as He spoke them to me: *"The witness resounding between Heaven and Earth," "The Word became flesh; the flesh became Word," "And God said; and man said," "Time is short," "1 (one) is missing,"* and *"In the beginning."*

When I looked at 11...11 (without the colon), it seemed like 2 and 2. That would be *"the witness resounding between Heaven and Earth."* When I started thinking about *"1 (one) is missing,"* I saw 111...111, the Trinity on Earth as it is in Heaven! I knew God the Father was a spirit and the Holy Spirit was a spirit, so the only thing missing was The Word. Thus, *"in the beginning!"*

Just as the Godhead is the heavenly Trinity, so we are the earthly trinity. We must declare the Word of God as never before. It will never return void. When we have the revelation knowledge that we are speaking in unison with God when we declare His Word over every impossible situation, it breathes life into that situation.

ANOTHER POWERFUL VISITATION

I believe there was another powerful visitation from the Holy Spirit this year during Pentecost. Sometimes I look at what the enemy is doing to see what God is about to do. One thing that is getting to be popular with young people today is splitting the tongue. I know the serpent has a forked tongue, and I think that is just his copycat mocking spirit coming against the cloven tongues of fire that rested on those in the Upper Room at Pentecost. Instead of the cloven tongues of fire coming down to rest on those who've been in the Upper Room, I believe some are now speaking with cloven tongues of fire, two swords coming out of their mouths. They are speaking truth out of both sides of their mouth, declaring the greater works of God!

ARMIES ARE ALIGNING!

Not long ago I heard the Holy Spirit say, "Armies are aligning for Armageddon." I believe this is a dress rehearsal for the big one! I shudder to think about the multitudes who are walking around with an attitude of indifference. My prayer is that Jesus will spew them out of His mouth while there is time for them to get a wake-up call and get on the right side. I pray for the foolish virgins among us to trim their wicks and fill their lamps while there's still time!

The eleventh hour was the final hour for the laborers to come in. The twelfth hour was too late! I see armies being mobilized in these last days—Esthers, who will see the nations delivered; Deborahs, whose cry for extreme justice will change the laws of the land; Jaels, who will drive their tent nails through the temple of compromise; Abigails, who've been delivered out of abusive relationships and summoned by their King; Eves, who for too long have felt that they "blew it" so badly they could never be used by God again. I see great armies of women who will not back down, back up, give in or give up. They are marching forward!

THE POWER OF THE CALL

It was a great privilege for me to personally participate, through prayer and fasting, in the what was known as "The Call." Held in Nashville on July 7, 2007 (07/07/07), there thousands stood in the gap, fasting and praying for forty days for our nation. Lou Engles received and answered this call, receiving the mandate from God and calling forth an army. Only Heaven itself will reveal the impact his obedience made on our nation and the world. If you're willing to be obedient to God's call, He'll give you the connections and the resources to complete your assignment every time!

Although I was not able to physically be in Nashville on July 7th, I was there two days later. I know it was no accident I'd had to reschedule my vacation for that week, even before I knew anything about The Call.

Arriving in Nashville, I sensed the presence that was still lingering. How friendly and happy everyone appeared to be! There was a peace that simply could not be explained.

Another very dear friend, Deb Reed, was also in Nashville that week. As I have noted before, Deb and Donna have one of the most unusual ministries I've ever known for two women who've never received formal education at a Bible seminary. Deb is a powerful apostle who has a unique calling on her life to set things in order for Donna to call forth the prophetic. They both have a great passion for this generation of youth and for Native Americans.

THE ANNIVERSARY OF DAVID'S BIRTH

As I thought about being in Nashville for the anniversary of my first son's birth (July 12th), I saw a remnant of children I believe God has been preserving. I prayed for and called forth this core for Christ to be birthed in Nashville. My precious David went home to be with the Lord just sixteen days after he was born in July of 1962. It's now been forty-six years since he left us, but my love for him grows stronger and brighter each year.

A STRANGE DREAM

I fell asleep briefly on July 11th, while Lauren and Elizabeth were playing in the swimming pool at the hotel where we were staying, and I had a strange dream. It was about a beautiful, blue-eyed blond named Chris.

Chris was three years old, and we were standing together in what appeared to be a mall. It was very bright, as if the sun was shining directly overhead through a skylight. When I laid my hand on Chris' head to pray for him, he said, "The nations." I awoke while I was thanking the Father for his wisdom beyond years. I'm praying this was confirmation of what God is doing with children, even the younger ones: *"out of the mouth of babes ..."* (Psalm 8:2).

A RECENT PROPHECY

The recent prophecy released by Bill Hamon, "2008 Is the Beginning of the Third and Final Apostolic Reformation," should make every believer so excited they will purpose to become overcomers who reign with Christ here on Earth! God's clarion call to the Church is this: "It's the time to give all of our life and labor to be co-workers together with Christ in demonstrating and enforcing His Kingdom in all the earth." Will you answer that call?

God is calling today. Is your phone line busy? Is your caller I.D. showing you Who's calling? Don't let the call go to voice-mail because you're too busy to answer Him today. *"To-day if ye will hear his voice, harden not your hearts, as in the provocation"* (Hebrews 3:15). There's a danger in avoiding God's calling. It can result in a hardened heart. Will you answer the call? There's a call to all from God!

It's time to accept *The Bride's Manifesto.*

My Prayers for You

For Personal Salvation:

Dear Father,
I know You are there, even though I have lived my life
as though You didn't exist at all. Please forgive me for
all my sinful and prodigal ways. I need You. Please come
in and change me. Make me the way You intended me
to be. Allow me to live for You and to bring You praise,
honor and glory.
Thank You for sending Your only Son, Jesus, to pay the
supreme price for my salvation. And thank You, Jesus,
that You came and did this for me. Now I want You to
be the Lord of my life.

Amen!

For Salvation for others:
(Place their name in the blank as you pray.)

Dear Father,
I know You are there for _____, even though
_____ has lived his/her life as though You didn't
exist at all. Please forgive _____ for all his/her
sinful and prodigal ways. _____ needs You, so
please come in and change his/her heart. Make
_____ the way you intended him/her to be. Al-

191

low _____ to live for You and to bring You praise, honor and glory.

Thank you for sending Your only Son, Jesus, to pay the supreme price for _____'s salvation. And thank You, Jesus, that You came and did this for _____. I pray that _____ will now desire for you to be the Lord of his/her life.

Amen!

FOR DELIVERANCE:

Jesus, my Savior and my Lord,
My soul is imprisoned, bound and fettered. Only You can set me free. I willingly renounce all spirits that I have allowed to control my life, thoughts and actions. I cast them from me—even from my surroundings. I now declare my freedom and walk in it, protected by the blood of the Lamb and the word of my testimony.

Amen!

FOR SICKNESS:

Jesus,
My body is under siege from sickness and affliction. You allowed the stripes to be laid on Your back for my healing, and You allowed Yourself to be bruised for my iniquities that were passed down from my forefathers. You did all this so that I can be healed and set free.

Jesus, I am so grateful that You did this for me. I will now arise and declare that I am healed and made whole in Your name, and by Your blood.

Amen!

MY BEAUTIFUL BRIDE

My child, I knew you in your mother's womb;
It was for you I was buried in a borrowed tomb.

Though many were the nights you softly cried;
For you alone I would have gladly died.

In your storms, valleys and fires, I was always there
To give you a testimony for others to share.

My plans for you are always for your good,
Even when they don't work as you think they should.

Remember, dear child, My ways are not your ways;
My best for you will be revealed in the upcoming days.

The Bridegroom is preparing for His beautiful Bride;
So finish this furnace where you're being purified.

This is the wedding rehearsal you've awaited many years;
Trim your wicks! Don't be left behind with only your tears.

My precious child, my heart longs for you, so do not tarry;
Put on your garment of praise, for My Son you shall soon
marry.

My beautiful Bride, always remember, for you alone I died;
So forget your past failures, for to you the enemy lied!

Genevah
November 25, 2007

Ministry Page

You may contact the author in any of the following ways:

Mail

Genevah Ministries
P.O. Box 130
Douglasville, GA 30133

On the Web

www.thebridesmanifesto.com
www.myspace.com/thebridesmanifesto

E-mail

genevahministries@live.com
thebridesmanifesto@live.com

Genevah Childers

678-402-8582 (N)

770-447-5547 (W)

235 Silver Ridge Dr.
Dallas, GA 30157